In Safe Hands
facilitating service learning in schools in the developing world

edited by Jean Clarkson, Phil Bamber and Lorna Bourke

Trentham Books

Stoke on Trent, UK and Sterling, USA

Trentham Books Limited
Westview House   22883 Quicksilver Drive
734 London Road   Sterling
Oakhill   VA 20166-2012
Stoke on Trent   USA
Staffordshire
England ST4 5NP

© 2008 Hope One World (HOW) Liverpool Hope University, UK

First published 2008

1005309364

British Library Cataloguing-in-Publication Data
A catalogue record for this book is available from the British Library

ISBN: 978 1 85856 416 6

Designed and typeset by Trentham Print Design Ltd, Chester and printed in Great Britain by Cromwell Press Ltd, Trowbridge.

In Safe Hands
facilitating service learning in schools in the developing world

Contents

Prologue
HOW Reflection

Keith Paterson

Going down memory lane, I must say that the close and fruitful partnership with Hope One World (HOW) at Liverpool Hope University, UK, has been and continues to be one of the most meaningful educational development associations that the Tibetan Children's Villages (TCV), India has ever had. A host of fine tutors have come to support our educational work for Tibetan children for the last 20 odd years: indeed too many to mention the names one by one. (Nawang Dorjee, Education Director for the Tibetan Children's Villages, India)

I t all started in the early 1980s with the opening of the World Development Studies Centre in October 1980 providing a new trigger for world development interests, not just at Liverpool Hope University but also in the local community with the Merseyside World Development Project and Justice and Peace Diocesan groups. As in all new initiatives it takes strong commitment in the early phases to ensure that there are strong foundations for future growth and development. S. Maura Carroll SND, Vice Principal of Christ and Notre Dame College (a founding college of Liverpool Hope University) provided this impetus. Staff involvement was required to conduct feasibility studies in Africa, South America (Professor Bill Chambers in 1982) and Mexico (Dr Keith Paterson). The first student placement project was in the summer of 1983 to the so-called justice ranch, Los Ninos, on the Mexican/Californian border. The focus was on working with orphaned children, especially those living on rubbish dumps and shanty areas in the Mexican border town of Tijuana. In 1984 Ralph Jones, Head of Science providing practical courses in science pedagogy for thirteen and fifteen teachers, respectively, in Piura and Lima, Peru.

The headteacher Mr Thakchoe leads his teachers as they complete the 'water challenge' during a workshop on building teams Tibetan Homes Foundation, Rajpur, Uttaranchal, India.

By 1984 there was a clear commitment to these activities and an embryonic infrastructure. The Third World Development Group held regular meetings, had the support of both the academic board and the governing council and links were made with local projects and people abroad. This early work was founded on the belief that we should raise awareness of global problems through the process of learning from the developing world and 'conscientisation', reflection on justice and peace issues. Sending students abroad for a third world experience and staff involvement with their expertise were seen as ways to underpin this vision.

One of our former students, Paddi Pearson-New, now deceased, had visited the remote Ladakh region of Northern India and drawn our attention to the needs of the Tibetan communities, particularly concerning education. Mr Dorjee continues the story:

The Hope One World group came into existence because of initial contacts between TCV, India and Liverpool Hope University with the financial assistance from SOS, UK (SOS Children's Villages). Dr Keith Paterson visited us from the UK and did a survey of our educational needs in September, 1987. The actual in-service workshops and visits started with Professor Alf Anderson conducting a science workshop at TCV, Dharamsala and Ladakh. Thereafter, tutors have come to our villages and schools practically every year to conduct workshops for about ten days annually in various academic subjects depending on our needs.

What emerged from my visit was a proposal for a four year model with one key subject each year, science, maths, English and education for Hope staff to be involved in for the professional development of the local teachers and schools. At the same time, students could be involved in working in the schools and villages. This simple model continues to be the mainstay of the work of HOW in 2007 although new variants arose based on local needs. As Mr Dorjee further reflects:

In time, the association deepened and widened in several areas: we fine-tuned the workshop programs from the formal settings to actually going to the schools and making a difference to the individual teachers by observing their lessons, giving feedback, giving sample lessons and informal discussions in small groups to interact on pedagogy. A couple of scholarships under the title The Tibetan Scholarship to study at Liverpool Hope University was initiated by HOW in June, 2001, and this greatly enhanced the capacity of our selected leaders from TCV. I hope this scholarship program as envisaged will continue. And now we have an invitation by HOW to attend the Big Hope Congress from June 4-11, 2008 in Liverpool. We have selected ten young leaders to attend the same and I am sure they will benefit immensely from this experience in England.

From the initial science workshop undertaken by Alf Anderson in Ladakh in 1988 for TCV teachers there have been many offerings involving staff and students in different locations in the Indian sub-continent, as well as in Africa and South America. As a result almost 2,000 teachers have been helped in refugee and needy communities. Twenty thousand or more children's lives have been touched and supported in their education. In recognition of the success of this work and as a fine example of international outreach, the university was awarded the Queen's Anniversary Prize for Higher Education in 1996.

The recognition of the contribution made by HOW is continued by Mr Dorjee:

Pupils from Tibetan Homes Foundation students, Rajpur, Uttaranchal, India.

Over the years, the close collaboration has blossomed into one of trust and mutual respect. The tutors who have come so far are of the highest calibre and are passionately dedicated to their teaching profession. Moreover, all who have come have found an intimate resonance with our mission and the work we do in our children's villages and schools around India, and have come to love our children and co-workers. We, on our part, deeply appreciate their support and are grateful for enriching us in so many ways, both personally and professionally.

According to our Buddhist philosophy, change is permanent and at a subtle level all that is compositional changes constantly from moment to moment. Therefore, on a personal note, I have been working in the TCV, India for the last 31 years. Come January 1, 2008, I have been assigned to plan and start our first Tibetan College at Bangalore by July, 2008. Do extend the same support to the next TCV Director of Education when he takes over. I hope this beautiful collaboration will continue in the years ahead and widen further even in our college project.

However, this has not been a one way project, now spanning two decades, based on giving: Hope as an institution and the participants involved have been beneficiaries too. Since 1987 around 250 staff and 150 students have participated in a HOW project. The personal enrichment for individuals has been significant. Everyone involved has their own journey to describe and for some it has been a life changing experience. Besides wonderful friendships and a much deeper appreciation of culture, the need to respond to those living in less privileged circumstances and the importance of challenging issues of equity and justice, are reported by many on their return. Staff have developed teaching materials and have integrated much of it into their academic work. Research projects tied to specific interests have also been completed. The case studies presented here are testimony to the vigour and productiveness of the engagement of participants.

In today's global village we cannot ignore other people's problems. Despite over 60 years of foreign aid and overseas development policy, there is a widening gap between the world's haves and have nots and millions still lack the basic needs of water, food, shelter and education. This book is testimony to one institution's attempt to make a difference in the field of education. By focusing on what we can do in our own limited way, we can claim to have made a small contribution to helping others in more difficult circumstances. In doing so we have gained so much ourselves.

Using technology to enhance teaching and learning at Tibetan Homes Foundation, Rajpur, Uttaranchal, India.

Introduction

Phil Bamber

'But you are no ordinary UK citizen, because you have come here to Malawi.' (Chief Maliri, 2007 in conversation with the Hope One World team in Lilongwe)

HOW was born out of the concerns of staff and students in a higher education institution to promote action for social justice. Sustained contributions to partner communities overseas have been made leading to outcomes that cannot have been envisaged by its founders. As might be expected, this work has challenged and changed the lives of numerous people in the UK and overseas. This book is written by experienced educators, with contributions from the students that accompanied us and the partners whom we visit. It illustrates how these experiences have enabled us to think beyond the possibility of creating a more equitable and sustainable planet: elevating our expectations for, and confidence in, the role we might play as the active global citizens envisaged by Chief Maliri.

We begin by setting out the vision, values and guiding principles of HOW. Our understanding of the ways our contribution can make a positive difference has evolved over time: it has been necessary to develop and articulate this shared vision to nurture coherence and a common purpose. This chapter presents the background to this extraordinary story and explores the importance of the interplay between social justice in context, partnership and learning to this work.

Values and guiding principles

HOW believes in the power of education to achieve positive and lasting change. Three values are central to the way we work: social justice, partnership and learning. These are extended into our guiding principles:

■ We believe in the power of shared endeavour to generate learning, to transform lives and to strengthen people's capacity to sustain action towards a fairer world

■ We recognise that service to others is an important dimension in the spiritual development of individuals and institutions

■ We believe in being openly accountable for our work

■ We value sustainable relationships within and between communities at home and overseas

■ We strive to embody a spirit of reciprocity, openness, mutual respect and integrity in these relationships

■ We believe the needs of the partners should be heard and responded to

■ We recognise the importance of learning from and trusting each other, of receiving as well as giving

■ We will learn from the skills, knowledge and understanding gained from experience

■ We recognise the importance of challenging our learning and broadening it to include the learning generated by service to others

Social justice in context

Liverpool Hope University is situated in the north west of England and has a strong Christian ethos, both historically and in the present day. It has developed as an amalgamation of three church colleges: Christ College and Notre Dame which are both Catholic colleges and S. Katharine's, an Anglican college. They joined together in 1980 to form an ecumenical college through the inspirational leadership of Catholic and Anglican Church leaders in Liverpool. It is the only ecumenical university in Europe, with a mission to provide educational opportunities for people of all faiths and beliefs, particularly where this has been denied.

It has been suggested that faith-based higher education institutions in the UK are more likely to develop distinctive and sustainable approaches to learning and working with community partners (Annette, 2005). Nevertheless, HOW is unique in the way it draws upon the human resources of the university to support communities around the world. As Liverpool Hope University's overseas education charity, it continues to be regarded as an aspect of life at the university that reflects the institution's commitment to its mission and values. The charity has enjoyed a high profile where a broad alliance has been established between those who have been able to make various contributions. Members of both support and academic staff have contributed through payroll giving or by sponsoring the work of SOS. Evidence of the extent to which both staff and students are attracted to the university by the work of HOW is anecdotal but appears to be significant.

The impact of HOW activity has extended beyond those directly involved. There are multiple benefits of embracing an inclusive approach. Julius Nyere, the late President of Tanzania, famously called upon leaders in the western world to spend their aid budgets on changing public opinion in their own countries. Organisations that work across cultures have a responsibility to portray the contexts in which they work accurately and be accountable for the work they do. An appreciation of the importance of improving understanding of development issues has driven the emergence of Development Education as an academic field in its own right. This inspired the formation of the HOW student group of volunteers for those who did not take part in projects. They use opportunities in the university calendar such as One World Week and Foundation Hour to raise funds and to promote awareness of the work of the charity. Their work complements the actions of those who have volunteered overseas.

This enables HOW to challenge myths of elitism associated with global citizenship: an underlying principle has been that first-hand experience of global issues through travel and work in developing countries must not be a necessary condition for staff and students to be involved. In the 1990s HOW programmes were publicised using the strap line 'From Toxteth to Tibet'. This made explicit the charity's attempts to link the global with local action: making the connection between voluntary activity in a district of Liverpool with the homeland of a refugee community in India with which it works.

Questions of effective continuing professional development (CPD) in cross-cultural settings are of contemporary concern. Several accounts within this book illustrate a commitment to develop CPD opportunities

Ceremony to mark the end of a workshop at Tibetan Homes Foundation, Mussoorie, Uttaranchal, India.

which are sensitive to disparate contexts which range from the training of teachers against a backdrop of the dramatic economic and technological development of India (Clarkson, Chapter One) to an education system which evolved under the shadow of apartheid (Hassan, Chapter Three). To sustain appropriate activity within a framework of social justice in communities across three continents makes it important to have an organisational commitment to recognising the relationship between effective learning and context.

Chapters one and two (Hankin) explore the student teacher views about their profession in the Notre Dame Teacher Training College in Bangalore, India and Akure, Nigeria, respectively. Chapter two also contains an analysis of the beliefs held in The Mountains of the Moon University, Fort Portal, Uganda. The respective roles of student and teacher vary widely between cultures and education systems: a failure to recognise these differences can result in damaging misunderstandings.

Partnership

Sustaining meaningful partnerships internationally is a concern for educational institutions across the world. In the UK the government's international strategy for education, skills and children's services (DfES, 2004) emphasises the duty, responsibility and obligation to support the improvement of education in developing countries whilst internationalising education in the UK. This has led to funding for specific initiatives such as Developing Partnerships in Higher Education and the International School Award. Both demand long-term links, underpinned by a principle of reciprocity to be maintained across cultures. We have achieved this by paying close attention to nurturing those relationships within and between communities, institutions and individuals.

The combination of support from the university and a major charity, SOS Children's Villages UK, as well as other donors has facilitated continuity and growth and ensured that HOW has had more than a localised and transitory impact. Initial projects in the name of the Third World Group provided work more closely aligned to a relief model: staff and students from the UK would teach in classes that did not have a teacher and supply materials to schools that were resource poor. Changing local context and continuity of experience has supported a move to an explicit focus on developmental objectives. There has been criticism that much research and educational development work in the developing world is directed by the donor's agenda. Our university charity has worked independently and responded effectively to requests for support made directly from members of communities overseas.

The Sri Lanka project (McLeod and Bignold, Chapter Four) draws on the expertise of the Early Childhood Studies team at Liverpool Hope. Their narrative explores the development of this project over five years and illustrates the local contexts that educators may have to account for if partners' needs are to be noticed and met. This includes understanding the expectations of the National Director for Education, of the attitudes and approaches to early years education within the SOS village and in the wider community, of the relationships between stakeholders, and knowledge of both the local and national formal and informal curriculum and the relevance of western research on play in the early years. McLeod and Bignold describe how they engaged with these multiple factors as this initiative has evolved.

Primary mathematics workshop in the Notre Dame Junior College of Education in Bangalore, India, 2001.

Hooper (Chapter Five) writes of his experiences in Brazil with two NGOs in Betim. He describes how a clearer understanding of how to maximise impact through a design intervention has emerged since the project's conception following a feasibility study in 2003. As a result, approaches to creative work at Missao Ramacrisna have changed. He concludes by indicating the strategies for developing partnership which were effective.

In Chapter Six, Cronin and Richardson describe how relationships formed during a project with community leaders and mothers in 2005 enhanced the outcomes of their project. They illustrate the 'primacy of the personal' (Chambers, 1997) in the approaches they adopted and in specific incidents. Bourke and Bennett (Chapter Seven) also demonstrate how the relationships formed by students can inform the perspective of staff and be integrated into staff workshops. These relationships with specific community members are treasured by student volunteers and have a significant impact on their behaviour as global citizens. Relationships between project members in often challenging circumstances usually endure beyond the overseas experience. The authors of these chapters advocate models of staff and student working partnerships as central to the effective provision of professional development.

This spectrum of personal connection has ignited and infused initiatives and partnership with the communities HOW serves, inspiring meaningful activity outside HOW's formal work. For example, the Malawi HIV/AIDS education project (Bourke and Bennett, Chapter Seven) resulted in a partnership with Sahir House, a charity based in Liverpool that supports people in the UK who are infected or affected by HIV/AIDS. In 2007, employees and volunteers from Sahir House delivered an education project in Malawi supported by a team from HOW.

Learning

The success of our work can be attributed to a commitment to learn from the skills, knowledge and understanding gained from experience. Grantham and Stevenson (Chapter Eight) describe the annual cycle of activities that have evolved to support the practical management of projects and the systems in place that ensure staff and students remain in safe hands through their preparation, delivery and evaluation of projects. This learning is presented in the form of practical guidance that reflects the value placed on partnership and an understanding of context. They identify the core unit of a HOW team: two tutors and two students who travel together overseas, and argue that this partnership is critical to the charity's success. They describe how tutors revisit locations with new members of staff in order to provide continuity and take account of differences between the locations in which it works.

Through the chapters we describe how we came to serve in each particular context, the type of work that was undertaken and the evidence of various forms of learning. The definition of service learning is contested: for some service to others is the primary concern while for others this is secondary to an academic approach which emphasises learning. For each distinctive interpretation of the term a plethora of service learning programmes exist at all levels of education, notably in the USA.

HOW is committed to responding to the needs of host communities and is concerned with what students and staff will learn from their participation. Unlike the majority of service learning programmes, students do not gain an award or academic recognition for their participation in projects. Our pedagogical approach, with its emphasis on learning rather than the traditional view of teaching, draws on theories that we learn through combinations of thought and action, reflection and practice, theory and application (Dewey, 1938; Kolb, 1984). It provides an opportunity to connect academic learning with the wider community, enhance the theory of our curriculum, hidden or otherwise, with practice and promotes engaged citizenship among staff and students.

The HOW model encourages student participants to process their experiences before, during and after their project. Whilst overseas they discuss their observations and feelings with staff and student members of their team as well as community partners: student volunteers are required to submit feedback and reflection on their return to the UK. This model of International Service Learning (ISL) is consistent with the definition provided by Jacoby (1996 p5):

> Service learning is a form of experiential education in which students engage in activities that address human and community needs together with structured opportunities intentionally designed to promote student learning and development. Reciprocity and reflection are key concepts.

HOW's model of service learning in higher education is more powerful and complex. There is an emergent emphasis on reciprocity and learning which is born out of a historical commitment to partnership. Sustained relationships between the charity and community partners overseas have enabled learning to take place that is genuinely bi-directional.

The contribution of and impact on academic staff ensures that HOW provides a model of learning through service in higher education in its richest sense. The charity has drawn on the expertise of staff from across the institution who share objectives beyond narrow departmental concerns. It has been able to harness and develop this social capital successfully. The tutors from the UK who have contributed to this book have first-hand experience of working with partners overseas. Their accounts are testimony to their own learning and to the considerable expertise that has accumulated for the 20 years of their service.

A study (Berg, 2006) based on interviews with staff volunteers found that they perceived their experience to have significantly influenced both their personal and professional development. The benefits for the university provided by professional development were in four key areas: enhanced teaching, increased research, critical thinking and collegiality among university lecturers (Berg, 2006). For example, projects have been linked directly into specific programmes of learning within the university: Early Years Education (Sri Lanka), Fine Art and Design (Brazil), Inclusive Education (South Africa), Education Studies (Nigeria/Uganda), Psychology (Malawi and India). Tutors also develop teaching skills which are transferable to their work at the university, such as developing a culturally sensitive pedagogy that enhances the learning experience of international students.

HOW projects are informed by research but have not been driven by a requirement to develop ideas. Nonetheless, the projects have developed the research and scholarship of staff: investigations into the psycho-social and emotional impact of disability research in Malawi, the transformative impact of service learning on student participants and the cultural and social barriers to online learning in Higher Education. Examples in this book provide further evidence of the four aspects in Berg's framework.

An appropriate response to changing contexts is dependent on continuity and learning: the education provision in the Tibetan community in India in 1988 when the first project took place is vastly different from what is described in Chapter Nine by Clarkson. In recent years we have worked with the newly established teacher training college in Dharamsala and a gifted and talented school in the TCV in Selakui. MacGarvey (Chapter Ten) describes the significance of ensuring that teaching texts are produced in the Tibetan language as an accompaniment to the increase in the availability of resources. Our understanding of and response to these changes is not superficial. Originally workshops addressed one of the four core subject areas – English, Mathematics, Science and Pedagogy – in rotation: more recent workshops have focused on more specialised areas such as the Teacher as Counsellor delivered by Judith Fiddy and Istra Toner in 2007. Edwards (also Chapter Ten) describes his experience of the new workplace model in 2005: his rulebook for new tutors is the latest contribution to this sophisticated understanding. He explores the symbiotic nature of university staff and community partner learning and the inter-connected forms and contexts of learning.

The demand is increasing for service learning initiatives to evaluate their impact and prove how well they meet the requirements of community partners both locally and for ISL programmes, globally. Capturing learning ensures the projects are more able to meet the needs of our partners rather than the needs we define. This should provide the impetus for those involved in such work to carry out research to assess their im-pact. This requires honest critical reflection. MacGarvey (Chapter Ten) asserts that this professional development work has a potentially seduc-tive nature: when we fail to meet our partners' needs they may not tell us so. Effective evaluation requires a thorough understanding of context, in-cluding an acute sensitivity to negative or unexpected outcomes.

One such unexpected outcome is a view held by some that the charity's *raison d'etre* is to provide material resources for overseas communities. HOW's contribution is more subtle: it is engaged with development work that has evolved from traditional charitable perspectives. Its work is in-consistent with a semi-colonial, paternalistic vision of the Third World. Despite this, teams are often asked to transport computers or large quan-tities of materials to partner communities, despite the often inappro-priate nature of these resources. This conflicts with the overarching aim of empowerment which underpins our work: it can destabilise expectations for educational development, reinforce a self-image of inadequacy and perpetuate a notion of dependency instead of the mutuality of our shared endeavour.

Bamber's interviews (Chapter Eleven) with student participants over two decades are analysed to find out exactly what they learned and what brought this about. He focuses on how their overseas experience has changed their underlying assumptions about the world. The unfamiliar is seen to help students question the familiar. He concludes that prepara-tion of students which is informed by social justice pedagogy with a formal critical reflection component overseas helps create the possibility for these outcomes to be transformative.

The exposure to difference afforded by their experience on a project is a further dimension for HOW. The research indicates that immersion in diverse and complex local contexts inspires future action. On their return to the UK, students have campaigned for the protection of Tibetan human rights, support World AIDS Day initiatives and set up school links between their present school, if they are now teachers, and the overseas community they worked in. The importance is emphasised of the approach of tutors and their capacity to build relationships with their team and facilitate student learning.

The work of the charity continues to develop through successful bids to initiatives such as the Development Awareness Fund (Major grants) administered by the Department for International Development. Alongside initial research about the impact of HOW on staff and students, this funding will help to provide a sustainable network of support for returned volunteers and embed a global perspective within courses offered by Liverpool Hope University. Meanwhile, Liverpool Hope University plans to introduce an award for students who volunteer in local or global communities and complete an accompanying academic component. This will draw on the knowledge, skills and understanding gained from the experience of Hope One World and provides a new opportunity to bring about positive and lasting change.

The book illustrates the ways in which HOW has responded and adapted to the ever-changing and complex landscape in which it works both at home and abroad and how its guiding principles have been lived out in practice. Consequently, it offers a model of service learning for others. And it captures our response to Chief Maliri's challenge: a challenge that requires us, and you the reader, to understand how we can act upon these insights to bring about a more equitable and sustainable world.

PART 1
Social justice in context

1

Education to service rapid economic growth in India: a discussion of education in a teacher training college in Bangalore

Jean Clarkson

Introduction

A clear understanding of the country in which you are about to provide service learning is crucial for effective delivery. This is not something that is likely to be acquired by institutions overnight and may take many years to accomplish. This chapter focuses on evaluations of workshops undertaken with over one thousand Indian and Tibetan teachers over the twenty years. It considers the effects of the development of the Indian economy on education from the heritage of the relatively affluent reigns of the Mughals and Maharajahs to its current global position. The overall aim is to recognise the appropriateness of the modern service learning environment within a globally expanding economy enjoying many of the available technological advances that have been made at the same time as trying to maintain cultural ideals.

The chapter reports research from a project conducted with the Notre Dame Teacher Training College in Bangalore. Despite my six year relationship with the college I am less familiar with educational systems in India than in the UK. In response to Hammersley and Atkinson's statement that the researcher who wishes to open up a new field of investigation has to 'break the vicious circle and negotiate their position into that knowledge production system' (1995, p67), I conducted a questionnaire study involving 82 student-teachers. It aimed to investigate to what extent future teachers are influenced by the effects of globalism in India and how the focus of the workshop can be adjusted in the light of rapid changes in the Indian economy and its effect on education in India in the 21st Century.

Whilst conducting the research it was important to recognise that the imperialist heritage remains a positive influence in the minds of some staff and students despite sixty years of independence. This positive approach aided and enabled the research investigation but the acceptance of all things British is a methodological issue. This is a common finding as Chawal-Duggan (2007) established in her research on accessing data for outsiders in research from overseas. The research in this project was conducted after the annual two week workshops in 'Teaching writing'. Thus a relationship had been established between the researcher and the study group in the previous two weeks which facilitated the process of data collection.

History

South Asia has always been famous for its trade with the west and is historically known as the richest region of the globe whose fertile soils give two and sometimes three harvests a year and whose villages are built on minerals. Dalrymple (2007) says that the dramatic increase in wealth in India over the last ten years is not an economic miracle or a surprising rise of a once impoverished wasteland. India before colonialism was a rich and prosperous empire with a sophisticated culture. During the reign of the Mughals and Maharajahs India was unparalleled in Europe for wealth and affluence. Palaces and precious metals and gems were abundant. Agra and Lahore were fabulously wealthy cities with populations well in excess of London and Paris. Dalrymple sees the return of the affluence and economic prosperity, albeit for the fortunate few of India, from a wider perspective and nothing more than a return of the ancient equilibrium of work and trade (Dalrymple, 2007). Yet currently Anglo-Indian relationships are still dominated by the memory of writers such as EM Forster and Rudyard Kipling, the television series the *Jewel in the Crown* and the news of floods in rural India. It is easy for university lecturers offering workshops in India to see the ties between India and the UK through the lens of the past and to underestimate India's current growth and its return to its former strong economic position.

The dichotomy of our preconceptions and the reality of India today is part of the discussion of this chapter. Its intention is to remind universities in the developed world of issues in the post-modern world. Workshops and service learning projects offered to schools in India by staff from a British university need to be mindful of the recent revolution in the Indian economy, be aware of the rich past of Indian's economic history and take into account the new generation of entrepreneurs who are growing up in schools and who will be part of India's future.

The requirements of the workforce in India have changed to fit the rapid revolutionary changes in the economy. The principle aims and essential functions of education in India, a growing, sophisticated, democratic society are summed up in three broad headings by Chitty (2002):

- schooling is a human fulfilment
- school is preparation for employment
- school fulfils a social function

In the past Indian immigrants to the UK arrived seeking a better life as restaurateurs, shopkeepers and traders: today Indians arrive as PhD students, software engineers and bankers. India's economy has expanded rapidly from an agricultural economy to a technological one just touching on the stage of industrial revolution. The economic engine is powered not principally by its factories or manufacturing but by the competitive service industries it supplies to the rest of the world. However the vast bulk of India's workforce still remains in the villages.

Economic changes

India has changed dramatically in the twenty years since Liverpool Hope began their service learning work with teachers in hill stations and tourist areas of India, including Dharamsala and Ladakh. The changes have implications for the focus of workshops offered to teachers in this rapidly developing country. Futurists agree that the speed of growth in the Indian economy will come to dominate the global economy. It is predicted that India will overtake the economy of the US by 2050 and there are signs of this burgeoning buoyancy and vibrancy on the streets in all major cities in India. As a frequent visitor to Indian schools over the last twenty years I find the optimism palpable. Dyson, Casen and Visaria (2004) report that

Workshop graduation. Notre Dame Junior College of Education in Bangalore, India.

India is the second fastest growing economy after China and note that the Indian population has the advantage of knowing English as an additional language. Thanks to this legacy of imperialism, Indian English is being beautifully spoken and written by Indian children in schools from kindergarten upwards. It is taught in a particularly English style, some have termed it *Daily Sketch* English as its formality reflects England in the 1950s. However, influences change rapidly, as this study shows.

In the last two decades Indian entrepreneurs have established successful businesses in their own country and used these as a platform to facilitate expansion into the UK. London is the natural choice because of historical and language connections. Today many Indian nationals are working for British companies in India and the interrelatedness of the workforce grows, thus creating the need for a contemporary school curriculum. India will provide the future workforce of the world with 1.1 billion people under the age of twenty five, fourteen million professionals and two point five million graduates a year. However, although India has 83,000 million-aires it still has 200 million people today who live on a dollar a day (O'Connor, 2007). The service learning workshops provided by Liverpool Hope must acknowledge the wide range of schools and children asso-ciated with this diverse population and ensure that the content of the workshops is relevant.

The India I visited for the first workshop in 1994 had one million mobile phones: today it is estimated that 100 million are used. There was one TV channel in 1994: today there are 150. The workshops offered by HOW in Ladakh, Jammu and Kashmir were for teachers who did not have running water: now they have videos, computers and, most significantly of all, reliable electricity. The taxis that took us to Delhi in 1994 were mostly Hindustan Ambassadors, the Indian-made version of the Morris Oxford. Today in the city of Bangalore which I last visited in 2007 and where the research study was conducted, the new flyovers and six lane highways are full of Mercedes-Benz and speedy Japanese cars. They squeeze alongside the auto rickshaws and emerge relatively unscathed despite the apparent chaos. These social changes are apparent to those of us who knew India twenty years ago and cannot be ignored. The preparation for employment as an aim of education proposed by Chitty (2002) has transformed the type of workshop provided to teachers in India by Liverpool Hope University.

Globalisation

There is a developing trend in all countries towards the global homo-genisation of culture. Films, television and the internet are spreading throughout the developing world and watched for longer periods of time by more and more people. Constant sources of electricity are necessary for this and the electricity supply in India has greatly increased its depen-dability over the last twenty years. Hindi films produced in Bombay are exported increasingly to the UK and this spread of a common culture through the media influences other cultural changes. The globalisation of fast food outlets was evident in Bangalore, the context for this research. McDonalds, Kentucky Fried Chicken and Coca Cola were previously re-sisted by India but over the last ten years have become ubiquitous. In the same way, it would be hard to find a town or city in the UK without an Indian restaurant. The overwhelming current influence in Indian culture is now from the US while India's imperialist past and English dominance is declining, apart from the English language, and maybe this is because it was adopted by the US. Coulby and Jones (1995) characterise this international movement of choice of cultural products and activities as postmodernity which cannot be stemmed by any democratic school curriculum.

Education is deeply implicated here. Stromquist and Monkman (2000) suggest that the curriculum in schools and universities are cultural and are influenced by the process of globalisation. How this impacts on the future teacher of Bangalore is considered in this chapter. Cultural and economic activity are not easy to separate. The English language dominates most global exchanges: it is the key to a network society and international culture. The global economy is increasingly more internationalised and more knowledge-centred. Changes in India's economy caused changes in society, not least education. The Indian education system has been restructured to include more schools where English is the first language of instruction. This reflects the changing needs of the economy. Nayana Tara (2007) states that the rapid and wide-ranging economic revolution in India requires the curriculum of schools and universities to be at the forefront of economic development.

Coulby (2000) proposes that technological changes in India have been significant and that their impact on knowledge has impacted on educational institutions and beyond. The characteristics of the knowledge economy through ICT and the internet mean that skilled teachers and technicians are needed to upgrade and maintain these networks. Teachers' skills must include the ability to teach ICT's manifold applications. The role of schools and the school curriculum in a knowledge society are part of significant social and cultural change as technological innovations have accompanied globalisation and impacted on human thought and behaviour. This can create social divisions because some schools do not have the finance or support to implement these ICT changes. Two hundred million Indians who live on a dollar a day are also oblivious to the major changes in Indian society. Access to the technology or the English language is not freely available to poor children: as a consequence Indian society becomes more divided. The ability to write and read English in the arena of computers has never been greater. Globalisation has significant ramifications for the world of education and the organisation of teaching and learning. The aim of school as a social function and the notions of Bourdieu and Passeron (1990) that schools are a means of social reproduction are relevant in a rapidly expanding economy. Social divisions are reproduced and compounded as access to the tools of learning are further away for some children in India.

Education and Schooling

Pandey (2004) reviewed research on teacher education in India and cited Singh and Malhoura (1991) who found that all studies pointed towards the irrelevance of the teacher education curriculum for today's India. The curriculum has since changed slowly but despite the prophesied doom of an irrelevant curriculum in teacher education the Indian economy has boomed. This parallels the industrial revolution in the UK in the nineteenth century and the premise that there was no specific educational curriculum provided that stimulated the economic expanse in industry. Economic success can happen organically.

Banaji (2001) warned that the education system in India was heavily oriented towards rote learning of unrelated facts and an unthinking acceptance of text book data and information to pass exams. She warned that there was little individual creativity and few free thinking teachers to develop pupils' curiosity, originality or criticism. She paints a grim picture of 70 children in a class and silence as the only appropriate behaviour: any form of unsolicited speech, even a question on the subject is punishable. She warned of the pressure to pass exams and the cramming schools where parents send their children. Discipline is strict and there is a pedagogical approach that values memory and facts over process, understanding of the concept and creativity. Nayana Tara (2007) investigated schools in three states in India and calls for an appropriate teacher training programme with post-training follow-up to modernised teacher education, to supply the demands of the technological society. In many schools she visited she found sports equipment and cultural activities locked away in store cupboards. She believed that the development of a healthy mixture of physical activity and cultural events were neglected in favour of rote learning of subject areas for exam success.

9

Notre Dame Junior College of Education in Bangalore, India. Workshop on investigative science in 2005.

Rationale

The rationale for undertaking this research was that as a staff member of a university offering voluntary service learning to India, I was aware that there had been massive changes in the schools visited over the twenty year period of our involvement. It was obvious that some of the environments of the schools were becoming more prosperous with a feeling of industry and affluence. I was aware that the school curriculum in India was fairly static (Pandey, 2004; Banaji, 2001): this was apparent in the school curriculum observed. However the rapidly changing world around the schools indicated that children required a more contemporary syllabus. India is destined to be the service industry capital of the world and the rising success of the textile industry and the performing arts industry in Bombay have specific educational implications. Western providers of service learning to the developing world sometimes equate India with negative concepts of poverty and lack of progress: this research hopes to expose this notion so that there could be a more fitting and appropriate understanding of the educational requirements of a nation that is destined to overtake the economy of the west in the future.

Workshop

I conducted a workshop for two weeks in how to teach children to write. In the workshop lectures and workshops were presented to 82 students who were on a two year women only, teacher training course at Notre Dame Teacher Training College, a Catholic College in Bangalore led by Sister Shanti. At the end of the workshop I asked students and staff to complete questionnaires which we first discussed with them before completion. The first section of the questionnaire asked them about their own qualifications, why they wanted to become teachers and how they thought teachers were perceived in India. The second asked them about how India had changed since they were children and whether they could remember differences in clothes, attitudes to gender, games and their personal autonomy and independence. I asked them to explain how life had changed since their parents were children. This was to show how life for children in the new India had changed and whether these changes required different educational provision. The third section of the questionnaire looked at what they considered were the major influences on society that could impact on education.

Students' views on India today

The questionnaires provided fascinating information about the students' thoughts on India and the teaching profession. Generally they believed that teachers were gurus and that teaching was a noble and respected career: teachers were the children's second mothers. However one of the more articulate students stated that 'although the work of the teacher is respectable some believe that the career of the teacher is low profile in today's India and some members of society think it is a low profession.' Key themes from the questionnaires are discussed below:

Changes since their grandparents' day

This section of the questionnaire asked students about changes that had occurred since their grandparents' school days. They said that a renew-

11

able electricity supply has enabled the ubiquitous use of technology, especially the internet. Students' grandparents often did not go to school and schooling was not compulsory, as it is today. Some grandparents wrote on slates as there were no pens and reported that they sat on the floor as they had no benches. One student described her grandparents' school as a thatched house. She went on to say that her grandparents were wise but not well-educated but that they were far more prudent than she is. One student reports that her grandparents' education was less democratic and more of a monarchy system. When asked to expand she explained that the teacher was acting like a queen in being autocratic and not allowing any interaction. She believed that teachers have better training these days but that there is still little interaction between students and teachers. For some children the education system in India has changed from the unsophisticated Guru Kula, an education for children who worked on the land in agriculture, to the modern system of English medium schools in the last twenty years.

Language
Students wrote that the introduction of international boards of education and the expansion of English as the language of instruction has been a vast change. Previously the majority of children were taught in Hindi.

Technology and mass media – globalisation
One student distinguished between a 'bookish knowledge and a technological knowledge.' She got most of her information from the internet, unlike her parents. One student at the training college wrote that the teacher training library was so poor that the internet was vital to training. The library in Bangalore is out of date and irrelevant to today's society. Most respondents believed that changes are due to the expansion of technology and felt confident that India has a big part to play in this development. Teaching methods have changed in India because of technology, the use of OH projectors and photocopying. The word globalisation occurred repeatedly in the questionnaires and students talked about how mass media had created a new demand for material things. The expansion of mass media had had an enormous influence on education: 'We sit in one place and we come to know about the whole world through a computer.'

Gender

It was generally acknowledged that girls have much more equality in today's India and education for girls is now compulsory. Some students from Kerala said that equality was always more prevalent in Kerala than elsewhere in the country. One student wrote that girls have many rights and freedoms now but do not know how to use them. She said that girls can walk hand in hand with boys in public now. Another student reported that women do not just want to be housewives now: 'They want to be independent. If we have our own job we can stand alone'.

Clothing

Changes in fashion are similar the world over: the equalising power of jeans, the universal uniform of the young, was adopted by most respondents, although they often wore salwar kameez. One student believed that the sari her mother wore was uncomfortable and restricted her movement. The influence of the western world and the mass media was thought to be responsible for the change in attitude to clothes. For special occasions like workshop graduations the sari is still favoured (see photograph on page 6).

Children's autonomy

Many student teachers in the group believed that children in modern India have more freedom than they had. Unlike most trainees in the UK who believe that children in the UK now are restricted in their movements and unable to go anywhere unless accompanied by an adult, students in Bangalore wrote that: children come to school by themselves now, which did not happen before. The freedom referred to is the freedom to choose what to eat and how to speak freely to their parents. They can do things and go places without their parents' permission. Children now have more opportunity to make choices whereas previously there was strict discipline and hierarchy from their parents and children were often afraid of their parents.

One student wrote that emigration had a major influence on children as they believed that those people aspired to a better life. Another student wrote that 'to get an education a child has to sacrifice his childhood so he can enjoy the fruits in his old age' suggesting that children must work hard from an early age to achieve results.

Influences on education

The majority of respondents perceived the influences of the new India as being the development of technology and the competitive spirit which drove parents to pressurise children to succeed in school. Having smaller families has allowed parents more freedom and comfort. Parents are perceived as giving in more easily to children's demands. One student observed that the education system had changed from the rod method to a free interactive method. Another student wrote:

> In old times lessons were monotonous and so many times we lost interest in studies but activities in the class and the use of teaching aids helped the children to be attentive. Previously there was a forced discipline, children used to just listen. Teachers were considered very high status because no-one else had an education.

Another wrote:

> Children in the past were afraid to speak to their parents. They had to do a lot of housework and help their parents in the fields and in the home. They did not give back answers and always obeyed their parents. This is different from today where children have more say in what they do and say and do not have the heavy chores.

Negative influences

Students in the survey reported that 'child labour is reduced but still prevalent and children are exploited in slum areas. Many girls in these areas are ignored.' Students wrote of the competitive behaviour of parents today which means that children learn a vast number of subjects. One student commented:

> Today's children have a burden of studying due to the vast syllabus and they have hardly any time for outdoor games. They are losing their childhood golden days in only studying and not playing. They need to be more free. They are missing sharing with others and they become selfish and do not share different views.

Another student thought that 'in the past education was less strict but now the standards have risen and it is very strict.' The media is considered to be a bad influence by some students while others believed it helped to develop globalisation and made children aware of worldly things. Many students wrote of the bad influence of computer games yet the technology responsible for these is what the affluence of Bangalore is based on. No one in the survey made this connection. One student suggested that communication was breaking down amongst children and adults because of TV and computer games.

Positive influences

There are fewer children per family therefore it was thought that parents are more involved with their children. However this raises the issue of the children getting everything they want: 'parents are very generous and satisfy the demands and needs of their child.' One student predicted that in the future that children will have a better and more comfortable life but that they will be individualistic and selfish. There will be less face-to-face communication and they will use mobiles and chat rooms rather than have conversations with each other.

Other countries

Students in the questionnaire wrote that knowledge of other countries and globalisation have had a tremendous influence on the education system. The UK and USA were quoted repeatedly as being influential to the development of Indian systems. Students also mentioned that international schools' curriculum were significant as they taught only in English and were concerned about global issues.

Childhood differences in the future

When students were asked about the future for children in India, they were generally optimistic about the continued growth of the economy and had high hopes for the children of the future and the education system. They expected children to be better educated than they were and that this would lead to a more affluent life. They hoped for good citizens and that India should be a developed country and people would earn more money. Being a good citizen was considered to be important: 'children should become good leaders, having all good qualities. They should be taught to love and serve. They should have a good family background which is full of love.' Only two respondents out of 82 hoped for a more equal India with poor children being considered.

Discussion

This survey supports Castells' (2000) research which indicates that education and economic development are strongly equated and that one is powering the other. This serves to make a society even more divided, especially in a country like India where access to technology is limited for some. Globalisation is seen to have an effect on the education system which is why the link between our university and the Notre Dame Teacher training college has evolved. Education is considered a valued commodity and all students at the college believed that education provided qualifications for a good job and subsequent affluence. Globalisation and economic development were universally considered to be a good thing as was emulation of the western world. Education was the gateway to power and the developed world was considered a positive role model. There were few reservations.

The internet is a key component of schools and universities for those lucky enough to have access to it. Responses to the questionnaires in this study indicated that ninety per cent of the teachers and children at the Notre Dame Teacher Training College and St. Saviour's school used the internet on a regular basis. The difference between the quality of the library and the information available on the internet is vast. Unlike libraries in British universities and schools, which are mostly contemporary and well-stocked, the access to knowledge through libraries in some Indian schools is impoverished and out of date. For students in India with the ability to speak English and to access the internet, knowledge from the developed world is freely accessible. The advantages are great and divisive. For poor children without access the digital deficit will prevent their rise through meritocracy. This reflects the pivotal work of Bourdieu and Passeron (1990) who warn that schools are a form of social reproduction: this is apparent in Indian schools.

During the two week workshop observations supporting Banaji's (2001) research indicated that students were unlikely to take the initiative and often afraid to make mistakes. There was a lot of rote learning and copying. This points towards the influence of their primary education where interaction was limited and there was a hierarchical structure. Children were not allowed to speak and rarely allowed to question. In the recent past teachers were some of the few people to be educated and therefore they had a high status in society that was unchallenged. The use of technology and free access to knowledge has given the opportunity for equal access to knowledge in all fields including education, medicine and commerce as long as you can afford a computer and have electricity. As children are given more respect and choices in their families they will demand further rights in school. Education and the modernising of the curriculum is considered essential for economic success and is valued by future teachers in India.

Conclusion

The chapter has studied the views of eighty two student teachers in a training college in Bangalore in the context of the dramatic economic development of India and the globalisation of education through technology. The following suggestions are offered for other educationalists from the west who will offer workshops to teachers in India and other rapidly developing nations.

Workshops provided to a developing nation can avoid some of the pitfalls that the developed world has made. However, attempts to review teacher education are considered in relation to the values and ideals of that country both in the past and present (Clarkson, 2005). The traditions of Indian education must be taken into account before change can occur. The movement towards free access of information means that interaction between teachers and pupils is freer and more democratic. There is less hierarchy. Pupils in India have further freedom of choice and are encouraged to explore free speech without the inhibition associated with making mistakes. Workshops offered by international agencies should encourage pupils to investigate using the internet and permit them to create opinions and use their own initiatives. Taking initiatives and leadership roles, especially for women, is to be encouraged and facilitated in workshop activities. Only a generation ago children in India were restricted to silent and repressive classrooms. Change will come about because having smaller families has given children rights and power that they did not have before.

Workshops offered to student teachers must emphasise how children learn using technology. Knowledge has broadened so that the teacher in the classroom is less significant and not the sole source of all information. The knowledge needed by teachers in the future, especially in a rapidly developing country such as India, is how to access and facilitate the many assets of technology, based on a real understanding of how children learn. The network society advocated by Castells (2000) is critical in the development of education. Workshops can develop the skills to access and synthesise information rather than memorising it for exams as in previous

Indian education systems. The key notion is that the global technological network, a constantly changing set-up, is potentially more responsive to contemporary social, political and economic demands: it breaches the boundaries of the state as well as the walls surrounding traditional cultural and religious communities.

2

Exploring African teachers' aspirations and the relevance of in-service workshops

Les Hankin

Introduction

U K universities have involved themselves increasingly in the education systems of African nations as part of their drive for greater internationalisation. This has been characterised by exchange and mutual influence, grounded in the 'common-sense assumption that [it] is good *per se* (Stier, 2002). The motives of these universities can conflict with policy concerns for global solidarity and with British government policy on Africa, said to be about damage limitation (Williams, 2004). Stier sees the virtue of internationalisation to be its potential contribution to a more democratic, fair and equal world, sparking a redistribution of resources by increasing awareness of life conditions elsewhere. Commerce is an increasing factor, as is a compulsion among universities to project their international social responsibility. This is evident from the educational membership of BOND (British Overseas NGOs for Development) and DEA (Development Education Association).

Much of this activity seems to act at the level of doing something transformative in a continent that is unknown and unknowable. Africa's fifty three nations, comprising ten per cent of the world's population, rely on others to portray them and a picture has emerged of a vast, ungovernable land mass that squanders the equivalent of all the external aid it receives on conflict. News of war, natural disaster and the malefaction of governments all feed the image of haplessness and compound the reasons for the west to interfere (Cramer, 2007). Many have questioned the motives behind this interference. For Chimamanda Ngozie Adichie, Africa is 'the place where the westerner goes to sort out his morality issues' (Moss, 2007).

All donor countries may have come up with just one tenth of the $50 Bn a year they committed to Africa at the 2005 Gleneagles summit yet there is still considerable financial as well as moral incentive for UK Higher Education to compete for partnerships with educational organisations in disadvantaged states. But what good is being done? The Africa Progress Panel, set up to monitor commitments made by G8 nations and the European Union, warns that sub-Saharan Africa will meet none of the Millennium Development Goals by 2015 (Africa Progress Panel, 2007). Whilst there are advocacy networks such as the Global Campaign for Education to hold governments to account over their responsibilities on education as a basic human right, no such groupings have emerged specifically to unify the non-commercial efforts of staff in institutions following a more personal, possibly altruistic line, where direct relationships are forged with specific communities for specific educational purposes.

This chapter enquires about the value of intervention by considering two different sets of experiences. One of these is to do with a workshop given by tutors from Liverpool Hope University, which raises questions about what possible relevance this activity has to the professional lives of a group of Nigerian teachers who are associated with a church school in a provincial capital. Notwithstanding the unmistakable and considerable enthusiasm such interventions create among those directly involved, can these projects justify themselves in the great scheme of things and can their outcomes inform future interventions? Another later experience is also considered since it adds to the picture of the teacher in Africa, beset by similar conditions. This intervention involved a single tutor working with teacher trainees in a new provincial university in Uganda, but asking them similar questions to those posed to the Nigerian group. In both cases the questions were used mainly to find common ground and to see what long-term training relationships might be formed. Talk of justification raises whole new sets of problems to do with the difficulty, or impertinence, of describing a much larger, if less successful, system, and inevitably doing so in the stereotypical and myopic ways that Adichie rails against.

In the predicted population explosion across Africa Nigeria will become the world's fourth most populous state by the middle of the century (Rice, 2006). Its education system is said to be impeded as much as any part of its infrastructure by a 'dire' colonial inheritance (Griffiths, 1995 p189). The most significant transplant from the British system may be the survival in the country's Christian-dominated regions of the church school system, 'transcendent' in spreading and sustaining school education through zeal, coercion, foreign aid links and determined community involvement but at some cost to other structures (Uchendu, 1993; Stock, 1995; Martin and O'Meara, 1995). The socio-economic realities that allowed the church system to take root may also account for the success of those interests now driving UK activity in the country's education structures (Mbachirin, 2007).

A workshop on pedagogy was conducted by UK teacher trainers in 2006 in Akure, Ondo State, Nigeria. The fifty participants described the workshop as highly successful. The very least that it did was to fill a vacuum in training that would be met otherwise only by publishers promoting their materials through in-service seminars. Given the broad spread of age and subject specialism among the teachers who attended the Akure workshop, questions arose about what forms of effective generic training might be of value to such groups and what the teachers themselves would regard as relevant for them, given the conditions in which they worked. What relevance could UK educationists have to this process, apart from serving to define needs against another system?

Background

The workshop was led by two tutors who had been active in HOW from its inception and who had worked together on similar projects in India and Africa. Nigeria was involved through Hope's tradition of supporting the teaching Sisters of Notre Dame (SND) who have a strong presence in Nigeria and across Africa and whose teacher training college was one of the founding partners of Hope. This dynamic church involvement has been extended to support the diocese of Akure, which is twinned with the Anglican diocese of Liverpool.

The awarding of certificates at the end of the 'Literacy through art and music' workshop Enugu, Nigeria, 2007.

The workshop was a path-finding visit designed around an in-service programme for teachers, most of whom had experienced little career support and who were working under difficult conditions: 70 per cent of Nigerians live on less than a dollar a day in one of the world's fastest growing populations where 44 per cent are under fifteen years old. There is an adult literacy rate of 65.4 per cent. Although this is reported to be in decline (Integrated Regional Information Networks, 2004; Education for All, 2005), what marks out Akure and other commercial centres such as Abuja and Lagos is a riot of English language signage that is striking for its grammatical accuracy and its expressive vocabulary when compared with the UK.

Conditions for teachers in Akure

The workshop was centred on the needs of the teachers of St. Matthias' Anglican High, a flagship school for the Akure Diocese and set in verdant, sprawling and underdeveloped grounds. The workshop was planned with the school principal, who offered the programme to other local schools so that a core group of over fifty teachers assembled for a programme that spread over one intensive week at the end of the Nigerian school year in July.

Any attempt to describe the everyday conditions in which these teachers and their students go about their work would be presumptuous, achieving little more perhaps than to illuminate 'something about Europe in Africa' (Wainaina, 2005, p94). Conditions exerted such an influence over the unfolding workshop however, that the workshop leaders were left to wonder, with Osaghae (1998, pix), 'what really is the trouble with Nigeria?' A recent academic review of the problems and prospects of Nigerian education catalogues the 'actions and inactions' of all the stakeholders contributing to the 'collapsing state of education' (Odia and Omofonmwan, 2007, p81). The workshop leaders were struck by the atmosphere of dilapidation, evident in the absence of public services, the unpredictability of the power supply, poor standards of building and perhaps most significant as an influence on children's educational success, rudimentary sanitation and unreliable water services (World Bank, 2000).

SOS (2006) sets out a range of colonial and post-colonial developments that might account for the visibly uneven distribution of wealth in Africa's largest, most ethnically diverse and potentially richest nation, beached among the twenty poorest in the world (United Nations International Children's Emergency Fund, 2005). Nigerian society is subject to a range of influences, many of which might be interpreted as factors in how these teachers engaged in the workshops:

> The World Bank's Voices of the Poor study lists the main causes of poverty as livelihood and employment insecurity, crime and conflict, and social exclusion. The poor generally face severe problems in access to public services, with women facing particular problems of lack of opportunities and having limited coping strategies. Persistent under-funding, especially for social services like education and health, has undermined attempts to improve service delivery and living standards. A major explanation for this lies in Nigeria's political economy – characterised by the excessive dependence on oil as source of revenue, and the neglect of other sectors such

as agriculture. This is combined with past mismanagement and what some external observers have described as 'psychotic corruption', which has denied investments in social infrastructure necessary to expand and improve on public services. (Larbi *et al*, 2005 para 2.1.6)

This assessment of national character and circumstance contrasts with the moral rectitude, courtliness and resilience demonstrated by all the teachers and their students who were involved in the workshop. This is clear from the statements they were invited to make to describe what made them special as teachers. Adeyemi describes his focus as 'to help the students to be their best for God ... to discover their potential and be fully prepared for the plan of God for their lives.' Iyamu and Obiunu (2005, p305) suggest that it is the responsibility of the teaching force to 'tap and harness the immense potential' of Nigeria's 'vibrant youth': educationists must fill the void and take the initiative, since lax parenting and an indifferent government have allowed the coming generation to 'veer from the path of moral decency and dignity'. The support of these teachers for corporal punishment, as their one guaranteed way of instilling civic consciousness and obedience, was the main point of divergence between their system and that in the UK.

The standing of teachers

At several points in our discussions the participants expressed concern about their status in society and their standing among the children they taught, since their acceptance of low salary levels was well known and they were perceived as lacking the courage to be venal in the fiercely competitive struggle for social survival. What is described as a 'sordid situation', the erosion of the traditional respect and prestige enjoyed by Nigerian teachers within their society, has led to low morale and self-esteem, high career attrition and a collapse in numbers of candidates for teacher training (Osunde and Izevbigie, 2006). These authors identify poor conditions of service as critical to the low rating of the teaching profession. Irregular and inadequate salaries, poor physical working conditions, poor promotion prospects and stagnation all undermine their status at a time when materialism has come to dominate Nigerian society. Since teachers' conditions mean they are not able to operate as freely as other workers, they find 'they are treated with disdain and lack of respect' (Osunde and Izevbigie, 2006, p465). This has led to such consequences as negative personal and professional behaviour among teachers and a poor attitude towards teaching among teacher trainees who are not shielded from the general lack of encouragement from the educational authorities. In the face of these conditions, up to half of all students entering the national teacher training programme may have no intention, even at the outset, of becoming teachers (Ejieh, 2005).

All these concerns are compounded for women in a country where sex roles are described as particularly rigid, even by African standards and where gender differences are culturally emphasised (Onyeizugbo, 2003; Davidson, 1989). No special recognition has been given to the condition of women by Nigerian scholars seeking to understand the country's under-development and endemic mass poverty (Onimode, 1982; Osaghae, 1998) but a general shift to increase their opportunities and access is said to be making some progress (Federal Ministry of Education, 2000). The practice of promoting teachers according to year of graduation has enabled women to rise to senior positions (Aladejana and Aladejana, 2005) and the experience of this workshop, which was set up with the female principal of the school, was that all sexism was subliminal but inviolable in that women were able to hold their own in discussion but would ultimately be expected to defer to men.

Studies suggest that teachers have not done much to improve their image and that they are perceived as 'stingy, guilty of inferiority complex, always complaining, shabby dressing and inability to assert their rights or project their professional image when necessary' and found wanting in the area of work ethics (Nwaokolo, 1998 p466). This public face has been filtered through a general perception of teaching as semi-professional because teachers have been forced to diversify and moonlight to raise their income. The stress brought on by this decline affects all educationalists in Nigeria in all aspects of life: economic instability is mirrored daily in the poorly maintained roads and rackety vehicles, experience of religious intolerance, job insecurity and the legacy of poor training, which leaves a feeling of inadequacy as a teacher (Ofoegbu and Nwadiani, 2006; Ogiegbaen and Uwameiye, 2005). One of the course participants writes despairingly: 'I think Nigerian teachers are lacking somehow, somewhere, here.'

Against this, the most recent version of Nigeria's National Policy on Education (2003) clearly places teachers at the heart of its ambition: 'Since no

Primary mathematics workshop Enugu, Nigeria, 2005.

education system can rise above the quality of its teachers, teacher education shall continue to be given major emphasis in all educational planning and development'. The National Teachers' Registration Council has
set out a code of conduct in order to find a way back to better times:

> Teaching is the oldest and noblest of all professions. The Engineers, Lawyers,
> Pharmacists, Medical Doctors and others are all made by the teacher. The teaching
> profession has more members than any other. These are unique features that make
> the profession the most indomitable profession in the world. Indeed, the history of
> education in Nigeria shows that teachers occupied the position of great honour and
> influence in their communities. They epitomised integrity, knowledge, leadership,
> moral rectitude and selfless service. They spearheaded the development of their
> communities and country. But over the years things appeared to have changed for
> the worse. In order to maintain and restore the teacher's enviable status and quali-
> ties, there is the need to enact this code of conduct to define the minimum stan-

dards expected of professional teachers in terms of their thoughts, words and actions. It is hoped that it will meet the yearnings and aspirations of the nation to build a veritable standard of education through dedicated, competent and dependable teaching force. (Teachers' Registration Council of Nigeria, 2005)

There is widespread concern that since Nigeria gained independence 'all forms of discipline, decorum and finesse have been thrown into oblivion. Laws are not enforced' (Ajayi-Smith, 2005). Nigeria emerges at the lowest point on international barometers of corruption (Transparency International Corruption Perceptions Index, 2006). Joseph (1996, 1998) writes of the 'dismal tunnel' in which Nigeria is stranded by its unique form of corruption, prebendalism, the conversion of office for private advancement which is so endemic that Nigeria has become a 'rogue state'. A significant academic and public discourse worries away at this open sore, exploring ways out of Nigeria's 'amoral', 'primordial' kleptocracy, where society is defined only by loyalty to one's ethnic group, a 'civic public from which rights are expected, duties are not owed' (Idowu, 2005).

Educational concerns in Nigeria

Among the issues besetting the Nigerian education system is an increase in the numbers of school-age children not attending primary school, at 24.2 per cent (or 23 million), significantly higher than in neighbouring countries (Iyamu and Obiunu, 2006). Factors discouraging parents from sending their children to school were poverty, value for money, fear of prevailing unemployment for school leavers and misconceptions about female education. The fear of crime and conflict referred to above is ever-present in the minds of the populace. And there is language:

> Every Nigerian child needs help to acquire literacy in English because that language plays many critical roles in Nigerian society. For example, English is a common language of communication among people from different linguistic backgrounds. It is also the official language-the language of government, the judiciary, most of the mass media, and commerce. Perhaps of particular interest is the fact that English is the language of education. Beyond the very elementary level of schooling, English becomes the medium of instruction and a subject in the curriculum. (Oyetunde, 2002, p748)

As Oyetunde points out, the National Policy on Education regards schooling as essentially synonymous with literacy acquisition in English, and being literate in English as necessary for effective participation in the social, professional, and educational life of Nigeria. He concludes that the government-run public primary school system has collapsed because few children learn to read within it and that, where they are able, parents send their children to fee-paying schools, which are mainly run by religious bodies.

The nature and structure of the workshop

The workshop on pedagogy required a programme with an open-ended and flexible approach because the needs of the participants would be unknown until the day of its launch. The workshop leaders framed a course structure in a detailed course handbook, designed to stand alone if all the elements were not covered in the sessions. This was then set out in PowerPoint presentations that could be adapted as the interests of the teachers became clear and as the physical organisation of each day unfolded. The programme had evolved from sessions that had been used successfully with Tibetan and Indian teachers across India and also with primary and secondary specialists in Malawi at different times during the previous fifteen years, adapted on each occasion to cover elements requested by participants. In this workshop there was a substantial section on techniques for the teaching of English.

The Teaching for Life workshop's literature is careful to root itself in the teachers' faith. For example, to find common ground and inspire it adapts a saying from St. Matthias, that 'we must increase the growth of our soul by faith and knowledge'. This worked well although there was a spread of faiths, including Anglican, Catholic and Muslim, as well as ethnic differences that did not obtrude directly but explained some tensions between group members. Setting out the workshop's aim to work together to learn more about ourselves and the learning needs of the students, the programme states clearly that 'these are ideas from another system: they are not *better* than yours but they may be *different!*'

With each session beginning with negotiating learning outcomes and ending with preparation tasks, the structure of the workshop was:

- Introduction: learning about ourselves, learning about our students, considering schools as being about people

- Learning: how do you/we learn best? Why do you/we learn? Helping children to become active learners

- Teaching: developing our teaching skills

- Organisation around classroom learning and teaching

- Resources: the classroom environment and display

- Speaking and writing English (the one firm request we received from the school before leaving the UK)

- Development and conclusions: setting targets, critical reflection, developing your career

These themes were sharpened when the teachers were asked to set out what they wanted from the workshops. Common themes come over most powerfully in the teachers' words: 'to gain more knowledge', 'to gain experience, good English usage and how to interact with the students', 'to gain from the experience of other teachers by rubbing minds together', 'to ensure that the students understand what I teach them so that they can stand among their equals.' There was concern for the needs of slow learners and talk of 'getting frustrated at the end of the lesson when the students have not really understood at all and it all seems like a waste of time.' What to do when 'students make up their minds not to learn' came up again and again. How to 'minimise student wastage' was a particularly heartfelt concern, which had several meanings: railing against the hopelessness of conditions, the indifferent attitudes of students and their lack of faith in schooling.

The workshop was also shaped by academic and practical considerations. For example, Maslow's (1943) hierarchy of needs, known to many of the teachers, was used to get some sense of students' expectations and to explore their self-esteem, facilitated through practical activity that drew on teaching and learning strategies such as circle time. The nature of intelligence was underpinned with reference to Gardner's (1999) views on multiple intelligences and opened out in activities on active and passive learning.

A sense of trust was established quite early in the workshops which was strong enough for the talk to go beyond the general to consider the particular conditions of the teachers' working lives. In-service support and training formed a significant part of this. How could it contribute to their effectiveness and the pleasure and financial gain they could draw from

their vocation? This discussion was triggered by a major government pro-
nouncement across the local media that training would now be provided
nationally for 140,000 teachers every year to rejuvenate the schools
system. Despite the weight of internal news coverage given to this policy,
we could not trace it when we returned to the UK. It went unreported in
the international press but sparked a cautious optimism rather than cyni-
cism among the workshop participants. To understand the relevance of
this and its particular implications for future professional development
provided by Hope, a survey was conducted at the end of the sessions.
Among the most interesting data which emerged from the forty nine responses were views about the government initiative and how this related
to the teachers' personal aspirations.

Discussion

The sweep of the in-service training proposal was a common concern: it
'would be good if it is well implemented. It should not stop at the training
level [but be] more encouraged through financial benefits'. It required the
government to 'put adequate preparation and thought into the training
workshop, as you have done.' 'Like this workshop, which put into practice
some teaching method which I have read about in my college days [it
should] develop into curriculum planning, the implementation of the
curriculum and analytical aspect of curriculum by the implementers. I
mean the breaking down of the curriculum into manageable com-
ponents.'

The criticism was realistic: the in-service programme would 'be a good
idea only if the government can also create more jobs.' 'To me the pro-
position is laudable but is the government sincere to herself not to talk
about the populace? [They] will be looking at the financial implications
when the time comes and policy will slip out of hand half way. [The]
Nigerian government is always propagandist. That is, the people in
government always politicise every programme or policy embarked
upon.'

Several course participants reacted against the government's proposals
for these 'far-fetched provisions'. 'One has sort of lost hope with their promises.' 'If they only stood by [some of] them this would go a long way to
improve the quality and status of teachers; improve the input and output

and surely heighten and improve the academic standard and performance of the Nigerian students.'

Nevertheless a sense of optimism shines through many of the responses. 'It is possible that those at the implementation level are truthful and faithful, dedicated to it. Our leaders must be focused and be role models.' 'This is a good step in the right direction. With effective teachers the Nation will be more productive and healthier.'

The Ugandan experience

These responses from Nigeria have many similarities to the views and yearnings of student teachers in Uganda and the conditions in which they seek to carve out worthwhile careers. These students were among the first cohorts to train at the newly-created Mountains of the Moon University in Fort Portal, western Uganda, where they were offered a less intensive version of the pedagogical discussions which took place in Nigeria. Commentators suggest that Uganda may be entering a new phase, shedding the brutal image of the past. Uganda was notorious in the 1970s and 80s for human rights abuses, first during the military dictatorship of Idi Amin from 1971-79 and then after the return to power of Milton Obote.

Having pulled back from the abyss of civil war and economic catastrophe to become relatively peaceful, stable and prosperous over the last two decades, apart from a brutal rebellion still smouldering in the north, Uganda has benefited from western-backed economic reform, generating solid growth and falls in inflation but has markedly failed to industrialise. The country has won praise for its vigorous campaign against HIV/AIDS. However no infrastructure exists: there are no reservoirs, no rail network and no municipal refuse collection so that refuse is sorted simply into what will or will not burn, with small fires everywhere. Electricity comes from a central hub down uncertain wires and is off more often than on. Despite the influence of the Universal Primary and Secondary Education initiatives (UPE and USE) there is no working structure of schools. A level of corruption is said to be miring the place in poverty and is much talked about.

Among the student teachers interviewed a recurring theme was the wish to be a 'job creator and not a seeker as it is for many youth in Uganda today'. Other ambitions were: to challenge attitudes towards teachers '...to work hard and attain a good class degree, to be able to share ideas, work with other teachers and to create a good feeling about the teaching profession to people who under-rate it', to develop personal satisfaction and esteem '...to be a great teacher who can easily give out knowledge and skills to other people' and develop notions of societal responsibility '...I want to do it leading as an example and furthermore upgrade my field of study, to be able to be ahead of my students: give them good quality information that can transform them into better citizens.'

An interview with the district education officer placed these aspirations and others in an uncertain light, similar to that in the Nigerian situation. Over the last ten years dedication to the targets of Universal Primary and now Secondary Education had led to the district still supporting schools with classes of one hundred and twenty children. There also remained a heavy reliance on outside, particularly Irish, support. Much of this had fallen away because aid agencies follow the movement of crisis and war and relocate to more troubled zones. Basic sanitation and privacy was a major concern with many girls forced to drop out of school because of the poor hygiene facilities, as is the case in Nigeria. These factors and others could have caused one student to reflect 'it would be better if I can also learn how to live in this world despite the challenges we meet.' Faced with other difficulties, such as the need to teach in localised languages, teachers were becoming less respected as they were forced to take on extra jobs after the school day and to teach in as many as four schools to earn enough to live. A quote from one of the students exemplifies what he would like to achieve: '... I would like to gain wealth from Mountains of the Moon University after my course so I can get money to build a residential house, buy a car and other human needs.'

This account shows that there is a clear role for outsiders to contribute through programmes of in-service training but that these should be part of a sustained package, negotiated with local officialdom but independent of it, with outcomes which are recognised as contributing to the teachers' status and rewards. The teachers are hugely encouraged by these interventions but expect more. In avoiding false hopes yet sharing technique and giving a sense of standards, these efforts may be a drop in the greater ocean but still have their own value.

3

South Africa: Inclusive education

Nasima Hassan

Background

Compared with projects in India, the South Africa project based in Port Shepstone, Kwazulu Natal is still in its infancy. Historically teams had conducted pilot workshops in 1999 in Special Needs and Maths and a follow-up in 2001 in Mathematics, laying the foundations for establishing partnerships in two centres; Port Shepstone and Bethlehem Free State. The locations were already linked to Liverpool Hope through the Notre Dame sisters and their social regeneration work through Pro Torkington, a former Dean of Liverpool Hope who had first-hand experience of the struggle to unpack the years of educational oppression enforced during the apartheid regime. Links were also established with Dr Justice Ngesi, the Director of the Department of Education and Culture which was based in central Port Shepstone.

The early projects followed a conference model where delegates from partnership schools travelled to a central location for intensive professional development. This model facilitated an exchange of ideas and teaching strategies, as well as providing delegates with the valuable networking experience. Lack of finance had influenced the decision to visit locations in South Africa in alternate summer sessions but from 2004 the project became part of annual strategic planning which recognised the need to include this vast country in students' experience and to solidify evolving partnerships. Rapid change took place from 2004-2006 with a shift in emphasis from conference delivery to school-based input located in deep rural settings, operating in the cluster model of in-service. Feedback from the second conference in 2001 indicated a need to support the implementation of inclusive education in schools throughout the region.

Inclusive education is a holistic educational philosophy which aims to meet the needs of all pupils, particularly of pupils with specific learning needs. The South African schooling system operates on a mainstream model for all so that pupils with special educational needs are integrated into the system. They are providing a cost-effective service based on equality for all, regardless of their physical disabilities, learning needs or other barriers to access. Despite the obvious challenges of this method, the inclusive education philosophy has been implemented in all schools in all sectors in the Port Shepstone region.

This chapter explores progress from 2004 to the present, with particular focus on the revolutionary educational developments which are taking place under the shadow of apartheid and also placing the needs of our established partners at the forefront of our work.

Our partners in South Africa

The Department of Education and Culture in Port Shepstone continues to be integral to our service learning delivery work in South Africa. Nombulelu-Yeni and Nonchlanchla are key personnel who have shaped the direction and focus of project work whilst maintaining sustainability, social justice and celebrating diversity.

Nombulelu, a former primary school teacher, school improvement officer and doctoral research student currently leads the inclusion team which facilitates quality assurance in terms of equality of access to the curriculum for all learners. Born and educated in the vast township surrounding Durban, Nombulelu is the epitome of active transformational schooling. Learners are motivated to value their mother tongue *Isuzulu* and their heritage *Zulu*. Girls, in particular, face the challenge of redressing the imbalance imposed upon their parents, so that a new generation of women can realise their full educational potential.

Nonchlancla, principal officer for supporting learners with hearing impairments has considerable experience as a school improvement officer and a special needs teacher. In 2005, the Department allocated its entire professional development budget to fund her attendance at an international conference in Brazil, exploring strategies to extend the learning of hearing impaired students. Subsequently, her research has accelerated classroom provision and inclusive teaching and learning strategies despite harsh financial constraints and an acute shortfall in specialist teachers in rural settings.

Project work in South Africa has also involved partnerships with a range of education professionals, including specialists in early years, vocational education, language and literacy and out of school learning.

Setting the scene: The legacy of apartheid

The unforgettable events of February 1994, culminating in Nelson Mandela's release, created an impetus for change in the history of South Africa. The statutory deracialisation policy, now embedded into a new constitution and education policy, attempted to unravel the destructive impact of apartheid. The Bill of Rights, a cornerstone of the new constitution, guaranteed 'the democratic values of human dignity, equality and freedom.' Section 32 of the newly formed Bill of Rights states that:

> Every person shall have the right to basic education and to equal access to educational institutions, to instruction in the language of her or his choice, to establish, where practicable, educational institutes based on a common culture, language or religion, providing that there shall be no discrimination on the grounds of race.

Subsequent legislation further challenged the apartheid era:

> in order to ensure access to education and the implementation of this right...the state must take into account equity, practicability and the need to redress the results of past racially discriminatory laws and practices. (Republic of South Africa, 1996 p134)

By reflecting on project work with the socially disadvantaged and educationally excluded communities of rural Port Shepstone, consideration of the legacy of apartheid was integral because of the recent memories of segregation and more positively because the realisation of a dream for these parents and young people we encountered was life-changing.

Educationalists faced a mammoth task in the implementation of the new legislation at classroom level. Sensationalised media reports of racial battles in schools reflected a wider national picture, where open defiance to the transformational strategy prompted the South African Human

35

Primary school teachers discuss their observations of a lesson delivered by a Hope One World tutor in Port Shepstone district, Kwa Zulu Natal, South Africa in 2006.

Rights Commission (SAHRC) to investigate racism and human rights abuses in schools (Johnson, 1998). Their conclusions uncovered the 'shocking and crude practices of racism, all the more startling because of its prevalence', resulting in a wave of academic studies into the extent of the problem and its potential solutions (Valley and Dalamba, 1999 p65).

Societal labels including coloured, black, mixed, mixed race, white, coloured immigrant and malay further heightened fears of assimilation and loss of cultural identities by parents in public schools (Soudien, 1998).

Fakier (1998) suggests that race continues to be a dominant dividing force with deeply embedded prejudices: this is illustrated by pupil interaction along the lines of: 'Don't sit by me, your blackness will rub off onto me.' Widespread research (Naidoo, 1996, Carrim and Soudien, 1999, Carrim, 1998) surrounding assimilation in formerly all white, all black and all coloured schools confirm the fear factor. Squelch (1993) identified the problems of emerging multiculturalism in education. Troyna (1992) argued a similar case from the British schooling perspective stating that due to institutional racism the likelihood that racial integration and positive role models would eradicate racism in schools was slim. Budget constraints, insufficient staffing and addressing widespread poverty meant that 'despite the rhetoric of diversity and choice the disadvantaged see little of it' (Valley, 1999).

In considering the socio-political climate in South Africa some of the wider issues challenging our partners are encountered. Their nature requires a long-term vision in order to change perceptions and to ensure equality of access: the leaders in advancing this change are educationalists and teachers whose task is to make the constitution a reality in the lives of all South African children.

Outcome Based Education (OBE): A step in the right direction?

The launch of *Curriculum 2005* in March 1997 signalled a new era in South African education reform as it went right to the heart of the ongoing process of transforming this country into a democracy and shedding the legacy of apartheid (Jansen and Christie, 1999). *Curriculum 2005* was a step in the right direction towards education for all, grounded in the philosophy of outcomes-based education (OBE): OBE is a learner-centred approach where the emphasis is not on what the teacher wants to achieve but rather what the learner should know, understand and become. Teachers and learners focus on certain predetermined outcomes. The outcomes are determined by real life needs, to ensure an integration of knowledge, competence, and orientation needed by learners to become thinking, competent and responsible future citizens (Botha, 2002).

The OBE model has been adopted in several international locations including Australia, USA, New Zealand and the United Kingdom. With the special focus on learner outcomes a telling shift in established thinking considers 'the quality of education and about what the learners actually learn in the classroom' as a primary indicator of academic engagement and success (Department of Education, 1996). OBE promotes interactive teaching and learning and the skills of problem solving, investigation, independent learning and creativity: it promotes the inclusion agenda as well as learning styles and theories on child development and differing rates of cognitive progression.

Many educationalists have commented on the revolutionary nature of OBE and its implementation in schools. The Chisholm Report on *Curriculum 2005* Review Committee (31 May, 2000) cited a need for ideological change in teacher training and a more measured, small-scale approach to the wholesale implementation the OBE model. The Chisholm report also provided concrete evidence of the grass roots reality, whereby schools continued to grapple with widespread, rapid reforms. As Singh (2000) explains 'historically black schools are under-resourced and their teachers under-trained. These schools lack the capacity to implement the OBE model successfully'.

As *Curriculum 2005* states lifelong learning; budgetary constraints and vision unsupported by resources is inevitably doomed to failure. The implementation of *Curriculum 2005* and the OBE model present a unique opportunity for systematic change and the improvement of quality in South African Education. The new curriculum contains elements of almost every innovation that has ever been tried in the educational field so that the challenges are enormous. Nothing of its kind has ever been tried on anything near this scale, anywhere in the world (Jansen and Christie, 1999).

Project work: From conference to school based delivery in deep rural settings 2004-2006

In 2004 a conference for primary school educators took place in central Port Shepstone entitled Inclusive Education: Theory and Practice. The five day professional development event was attended by fifty four delegates from deep rural settings. Many were in post as teacher responsible for implementing inclusive education strategies in the classroom. Most of them had the task of cascading the sessions to colleagues in their schools at a later date so that their attendance was considered a valuable long-term investment by the school.

Resources to support the various activities which took place during the conference were purchased from wholesale educational retail outlets in downtown Durban and materials for practical sessions were sourced in local markets and large retail chains which were familiar to local residents and also easy to get to. Luggage allowance enabled only the essential theoretic reference materials to be purchased in Liverpool. Sustainability of teaching resource ideas and materials was a major factor in planning the conference, thus it was a key consideration to make such purchases locally. Details of supplier and costing were circulated to all delegates, to further promote the accessibility and sustainability of the teaching and learning strategies adopted.

The overhead costs incurred such as travel to and from venue, accommodation, catering and sundries were all met by the Department of Education and Culture. The conference was designed to meet the theoretic and practical needs of the delegates, many of whom were engaged in post-graduate study with the University of Kwazulu Natal, the Rainbow University. Each morning aspects of child development and learning theories were explored, followed by hands-on activities which resulted in the production of materials to be used in the classroom.

Delegates enjoyed the professional engagement with the added benefit of being able to fully immerse themselves in creating resources which continued well into the early hours to meet the needs of the learners. Networking and the support offered by colleagues who rarely come into contact with one another were also positive features of the conference model. Daily evaluations explored how educators would implement the strategies introduced into their classroom practice. Educators repeatedly cited the acute lack of resources in their schools and vast pupil numbers as problematic in the successful implementation of inclusive education strategies.

Evaluations of this conference overwhelmingly requested workshops to be based in schools so that presenters became familiar with the reality of the teaching experience. This would be challenging as a large number of delegates came from a broad range of school settings from the well-established and financially strong to the newly convened and financially weak.

Mr SA Ngongoma, the principal of Enkanini Primary School, Port Shepstone, Kwa Zulu Natal, South Africa dances in front of a captive audience with local Zulu celebrity, Phuzekhemisi.

Before our departure we visited three schools, delivering literacy lessons at key stage 2, grade 3 and key stage 3, grade 7. This helped us to prepare fully for future collaborations with our partners and to become fully aware of the challenges presented in classroom-based teaching with an emphasis on inclusion. Furthermore, hidden costs such as carers and parents taking time away from family and home responsibilities and the disruptive effect on schools who could not provide cover for absent teachers further resulted in a change of format from conference delivery to school-based input.

2005: School based delivery

In response to partner needs a team of two tutors worked in five primary schools for ten days during the 2005 project in South Africa. The schools were selected by advisers and school improvement officers in the Department of Education and Culture to reflect the range of settings in the mountain locations. The schools were also selected to encourage clustering opportunities for teachers in the locality. Flagship pilot schools were included with well-established curricula and structures, accommodation and facilities. These schools had evolved over 25 years, surviving by parental and community-generated funding during the apartheid years.

English was the language of instruction throughout the schools, and spoken with great competence at key stages 4 and 5. Classrooms were a hive of activity and stimulation. The senior management teams for the schools and teaching staff were all fully qualified and the standard assessments competed academically with all white schools in Durban. Some learners progressed to university, depending on family finances. Extra-curricular activities included cultural dance and team sports in which the senior boys' football team was a regional champion.

Other schools were newly designated in remote communities which were less than five years old. To illustrate, one school is housed in former farm outhouses, consisting of a long corridor and empty rooms. Here learners sit on reed mats, often seventy to a class. Two teachers occupy each end of a long room, along with their sixty or so pupils each and no partition to speak of. There are no teaching materials or resources whatsoever. Some of the teachers are respected members of the local community with good spoken English. Teaching is by didactic methods with consistent use of the mother tongue at key stages 1 and 2.

Evaluations based on the 2005 school-based delivery confirmed that this was the most appropriate approach in supporting inclusive education. Travelling to and from settings involved lengthy journeys by car, sometimes on incomplete roads. However, this time could be effectively used to plan the day ahead, learn about the staffing issues in the school, address their specific curriculum requirements or discuss the amalgamation of classes so that more teachers could participate in the activities. Each day ended with an open forum discussion of the observations, resources used and classroom constraints. Personnel from the Department of Education and Culture were able to make recommendations for resources, further courses and organise clustering events during this time. Hence, there was a sense of progression and development with built-in review points to assess how educators were able to implement the strategies they had observed.

2006: Student engagement and school-based delivery

Building on the well-established links with schools in rural settings in 2006 the project was able to pilot student participation for the first time. Thus the South African project was running in a similar way to projects in India and Sri Lanka, with a team of two tutors and two students, both trainee primary teachers, planning school-based delivery. This decision was not taken lightly as it was more costly in terms of flights compared with India and Sri Lanka and the emphasis on school-based delivery meant that recruitment from initial teacher education courses had to intensify to meet partnership needs. This marked a significant investment by the charity in the ongoing progression of the South African project. By this time links with Bethlehem Free State were on hold due to key personnel being engaged in international work: our team of four would work in nine schools over ten days in Port Shepstone teaching literacy, numeracy, performing arts, creative arts and geography. Despite the extended curriculum we were still able to find and purchase all resources on location in Durban or Port Shepstone.

Once students had been selected, in accordance with recruitment procedures, intensive training commenced. The South Africa team then met to research, plan and review the specified curriculum areas which was requested by our partners.

A review of the lesson plans and resources was essential to ensure that inclusion policies were part of the tasks learners would be asked to undertake. Each member of the team produced a sequence of lessons on a given theme. Teaching strategies, materials, starters and plenary activities were all reviewed with sustainability and inclusion as primary factors. For our project work to have a long-term impact the resources had to be replicated in a cost-effective manner with limited wastage of funds and materials. Students later reported that this planning process had empowered and challenged them to explore creativity to a greater degree and to question the over-emphasis on ready-made teaching resources which did not meet the needs of the learners.

What did the staff learn?

The South African education system encourages parents to enrol their children in any school of their choice, regardless of their familiarity with the language of instruction: Educators therefore face increasing difficulties in supporting learners who are being taught in a second or third language. In the South African context, English is the medium of mass media communication and links to a more global emerging South African identity (Myburgh, 2004).

Maruyama and Deno (1992) explored multilingualism in primary classroom settings which reflected diverse catchment areas, norms of behaviour and learner experiences in formal instruction. They found that the learner experience of instruction in a language other than their mother tongue led to feelings of helplessness: learners viewed the classroom as a barrier and lacked self-confidence and felt isolated and even rejected. Learners perceived their language of instruction and the language they speak at home as two different entities. When speaking the language of instruction with friends outside school, they are ridiculed and labelled. 'At home the children say you are a coconut... you are going to change and be white people' (Myburgh, 2004). Nieto (2000) confirms that this perception of English is based on the notion that learners who are not fluent in English are handicapped as their future economic capabilities, social mobility and long-term welfare are linked to a competent command of English.

Many learners in partnership schools could relate to the issues raised in the multilingual settings. Though the schools celebrated diversity, the challenges of coping with a multilingual environment were also of a pressing nature for parents, educators and individual learners. A further challenge to educators is to be aware of and acknowledge the linguistic range, ensuring that different languages are given a place and valued in the classroom minimises feelings of alienation, conflict and academic exclusion. As the language of instruction in all schools supported from Grade 3 (Key Stage 1) is English, our project work is made easier – although it is hard for parents and carers who aspire to support their

children's education yet are excluded by their language levels in English. This hurdle is overcome to some extent by educators who provide after hours translation and support for parents.

This level of commitment to their work all adds to the honoured status given to the teaching profession in South Africa. Teachers have long been considered able to provide the route from poverty and deprivation into self-realisation and prosperity. This applies equally to teachers of academic and vocational education because the value of gardening and harvesting vegetables grown in the homestead cannot be under-estimated.

Service learning in partnership with the Department of Education and Culture is both professionally challenging and personally rewarding. Schools where the head teacher prioritised the nutrition programme, subsidised rice, milli meal, vegetables and meat to provide a hot meal in the day confirmed the reality of teaching in a country where widespread poverty is the norm. Providing learner, who have walked up to fifteen kilo-metres to school, with the only meal they will eat that day is without doubt meeting a greater, global need in terms of educational reform. En-countering communities ravaged by HIV/AIDS, with no localised medical

Participants in the 'Inclusive Education' workshop Port Shepstone, Kwa Zulu Natal, South Africa celebrate their work together in 2005

support and an increase in 'child headed' households mean that educators must forge strong pastoral systems before learning can take place. Some teachers involved in the project lived in shared accommodation close to the school building during the working week. After school, their role as life-long learning advisors to the wider community would commence. At weekends they travelled into Port Shepstone and beyond to touch base with their other family and community.

Both Nombulelu and Nonchlanchla actively promoted teaching as career options, offering professional and at times financial support to trainee teachers from the rural communities. They were given no guarantee of jobs: instead they were encouraged to teach in inner city Durban for a time to take advantage of the professional development opportunities on offer. They would return to their home communities as curriculum leaders and senior managers in due course.

Conclusion

Service learning opportunities in South Africa continue to expand globally so that an understanding of outcomes-based education is central to the success of future projects. Despite the many challenges facing the education system in South Africa, transformational educational reform has been adopted throughout the country, as illustrated by the partnerships established by HOW teams in remote rural locations. Future projects may incorporate a longer project with new and emerging schools across the primary, middle and secondary sectors. In addition project work in the 16-19 sector, with a focus on vocational education, presents new and exciting areas for professional development. Our way of working enables undergraduate students to have a meaningful experience of globalisation and internationalism in the fields of education and community development, as well as providing a unique life-changing experience in one of the world's most beautiful and promising countries.

PART 2
Partnership (models of delivery)

4

Creative project development –
An Early Years case study, Sri Lanka

Naomi McLeod and Wendy Bignold

I t was due to the success of the partnership with TCV in India that we were asked to consider initiating a project with SOS villages in Sri Lanka in 2001. The request was to target English language teaching in the five SOS kindergartens. This differed from other projects as it specifically focused on young children and their teachers. The Education Deanery at Liverpool Hope University has developed expertise in early years' education and care: an Early Education degree was introduced in 1998 and an Early Childhood Studies degree in 2000. Therefore, when the request came from the National Director of SOS Sri Lanka, HOW worked collaboratively with the Early Years' Team at Hope to plan a possible project. A feasibility study was conducted to establish a pilot project that would meet the needs of the target group which was 3 to 5 year-olds in the SOS kindergartens. This chapter traces the development of the Sri Lankan project from that point through the following five years.

Background

Sri Lanka has a high literacy rate compared with its neighbouring countries: it is just over 86 per cent (90.5% for men and 82.9% for women). This is evidence of the value placed on education in the country. Children begin compulsory schooling in the January after their fifth birthday and many of them start kindergarten shortly after they are three. State education is free from kindergarten to university. However, an increasing

49

number of schools are in the private sector, particularly pre-school provision and SOS kindergartens. At the SOS early years settings places are free for SOS children but there are also fee-paying children from the local community who attend: so while providing an early years' education for SOS children, the kindergartens also provide an important source of income for SOS Sri Lanka.

Many private institutions call themselves international schools, as they teach in English. State schools teach in the majority language, Sinhala, with some Tamil language teaching. English is taught as a curriculum subject at primary and secondary level and it is also popular in private kindergartens with many young children learning to speak, read and write in English. English is becoming increasingly important in the country and in the wider region of South West Asia, particularly in relation to employment opportunities. This was the main impetus for setting up an English language project. The National Director of SOS Sri Lanka felt that raising the standard of English language teaching in the kindergartens would give SOS children early confidence in English language and a firm foundation to build on in school. The introduction of foreign or additional languages in the early years is recognised as important for later language competency. English teaching is attractive to parents of young children in the community and increases the number of fee-paying children. This was never a planned primary outcome but will have a positive impact on the work that SOS Sri Lanka is able to do through increased income.

Approaches to the feasibility study

There is an SOS Kindergarten in each of the five SOS villages in Sri Lanka: they are located around the country with one centre in each of the main regions. The feasibility study visited all five in order to identify similarities and differences and focused on the following key questions which would be crucial to a successful project:

- What English language teaching was already taking place and to what effect?

- What might the structure and the content of the project be?

- Which Hope staff would be best equipped to participate in the project?

■ Which SOS kindergarten teachers would most benefit from direct involvement?

■ What likely impact would the project have on the target group of children?

■ What were the cultural sensitivities which needed to be taken account of?

■ What contribution could Hope students make?

■ What were the logistics? For example, which SOS villages/kindergartens would be involved? Where would Hope students and staff stay? Given the work commitments of Hope and SOS staff, how long should the project last?

This feasibility study was conducted by a senior member of Hope's Early Years' team who had experience of project management in Asia, in partnership with the Deputy Director of SOS Sri Lanka. Observations were done in the kindergartens and informal conversations were held with teachers and many other SOS staff who had direct contact with the children.

Through the conversations with kindergarten teachers it was clear that the level of English used by and understood by the teachers varied considerably. One early proposal was that this would make formal English language classes difficult for our students to conduct with the teachers. A more effective approach might be for the teachers to learn conversational English and topic-related vocabulary through interaction with students and tutors at workshops. The kindergartens operate for three hours every weekday morning. Teachers are employed for the whole day and are required to prepare the following day's activities each afternoon. This provided an opportunity for local teachers to work alongside Hope students and tutors in the kindergartens in the mornings, observing them working directly with the children. The afternoons could then be used for focused workshops in English but exploring general early years' pedagogy and facilitating the development of English language and the enhancement of early years' provision.

The feasibility study acknowledged that good practice already existed with some kindergarten teachers providing a range of stimulating activi-

A Hope One World student takes part in practical activities outside the classroom. SOS Children's Village, Piliyandala, Sri Lanka in 2004.

ties and experiences for their pupils. Although teaching methods varied slightly between kindergartens there was general uniformity of provision. This would allow for common themes to be developed in the workshops to the benefit of all local participants. Good local practice could be shared to the benefit of all participants, including Hope staff and students who could clearly learn from the local staff.

Play in the form of singing, dancing and rhymes is acknowledged as being highly valuable aesthetic education and an important part of the curriculum in Sri Lanka at every stage of education. Both children and teachers were observed having much fun doing these kinds of activities. However, when the songs and rhymes were in English it was not always clear whether the children understood what they were singing about. English language was taught mainly by drilling the children, both in written and oral form.

Some play took place in all kindergartens but it was formal and structured compared with early years' provision in England. The interpretation of play is strongly influenced by culture (Curtis, 2005) so that play was regarded as a pleasant activity for the children but was not fully appreciated as a vehicle for learning. Many of the kindergarten teachers fully recognised the value of play but felt unable to use it as significant part of their practice due to pressure from senior staff who did not. This raised the first major issue: How could we help kindergarten teachers feel more confident about their practice and be recognised for the experts they were?

It was recommended that the importance of play for young children should be the basis of the first workshop demonstrating methods to enhance children's experiences and learning. This was intended to reinforce and value the local teachers' practice and philosophy. The National Director was keen to run a full programme of these workshops to make the importance of play clear to senior managers. The study of play would also provide an opportunity for 'cross-cultural bridge-building' (Herbert, 2006), in this case the study of play from a traditional Sri Lankan cultural perspective and contemporary western research on play in the early years. This approach would value the contributions and prior experiences of all participants.

Local teachers were asked what they would like workshops to include to ensure that they felt some sense of ownership of the project. New ideas for art and craft were always the priority. All of the children in the kindergartens had their names on the wall with their art work hanging underneath. Each time a new piece was completed it was hung on top of previous ones. The children took great pride in displaying their work as did the teachers. However, there was potential for greater creativity to be developed in the children and teachers. For this reason it was recommended for workshops to be a mixture of theory and practical activities. This would also facilitate the development of teaching materials using local resources and games which would add to the limited resources in the kindergartens.

Student involvement
The majority of projects involved students from the university. As this project was focused on young children Early Childhood Studies students

53

were used as project partners in order to benefit from their subject expertise. They would teach in the kindergartens, facilitating the development
of English in the children and teachers. Being involved in a project like
this enabled students to learn from work-based learning, as discussed by
Sobiechowska and Maisch (2006). Work-based learning in this project
would be a general preparation for the world of work with the development of transferable skills which students would be able to use in employment in early years' settings. Being part of such a project also provided an
opportunity for students to develop as global citizens, nurturing their
global responsibility. This is arguably a role of education, particularly
higher education, in a globalised world (Hankin and Bignold, 2006).

Rebecca Dixon, an undergraduate studying Education at Hope, applied to
be part of the project. Unlike most other student applicants, Rebecca had
already had experience of living in developing countries. Indeed, she had
spent several months living in Sri Lanka, where her parents were working,
before coming to university. When asked why she wanted to be part of a
HOW project, she said that travelling with her family had given her a
range of perspectives on life and the world. She saw HOW as 'a fantastic
opportunity' to do something which combined her commitment to education with her experiences prior to university:

> Working as part of a team with experienced Hope tutors I would be able to learn
> from their expertise. Being part of a team with local people in their setting I would
> have the opportunity to take on their experiences. I wanted to share local ex-
> periences, to embrace their ideas; not to change them but to learn from them and
> develop them.

Students like Rebecca fully appreciate the opportunity to develop their
own learning. The student selection process requires candidates to
demonstrate this awareness. Despite having already spent time in Sri
Lanka Rebecca recognised that in working with SOS children and staff she
would be 'living a different life – the other side of the coin' from an ex-
patriate community member. She relished this; 'I knew I would gain a lot
from that, from working together with other people when you think you
have too many differences, that the divide will be too big.'

This positive attitude and commitment is valued and acknowledged. The
voices of students who are selected to be part of the project are important.
Their hopes and aspirations must be heard as well as their anxieties as they

are partners in the project and they are listened to. The Sri Lanka project students have particular expertise as they are generally studying Early Years' or Education and they have valuable, and often innovative ideas about how the project might operate and how to engage the children. Students such as Rebecca are crucial to the success of HOW and its work.

The first workshops

In 2001 two tutors and two students visited a SOS village in Sri Lanka. As many teachers as possible from the other four SOS villages on the island travelled to the host village which enabled the tutors to work with the kindergarten teachers using a series of workshops. As identified in the feasibility study the request was for theory to be underpinned by a practical element. The first series of workshops looked at how to teach English as an additional language in relation to early years' pioneers such as Froebel, Steiner and Montessori. According to Leibschner (1992) Froebel proposed that it is through play alone that children learn concentration: they learn to work for a purpose and to carry through and achieve an end which is worthwhile to them. Therefore consideration was paid to the process involved in teaching and learning within the kindergartens rather than just the end product. Discussions of why and how different approaches encourage deep and meaningful learning by children were important.

With support and guidance from the tutors the two students planned and prepared resources that supported early reading and EAL and reinforced what was being taught in the workshop sessions. All the activities involved speaking and listening and incorporated visual aids as well as actions so that the children would begin to understand what they were speaking or singing about and learning would be more meaningful for them. Vygotsky (1978 p24) suggested that 'the most significant moment in the course of intellectual development ... occurs when speech and practical activity, two previously completely independent lines of development converge.' This became clearly evident not only in the afternoon sessions with the children of different ages but also in the workshops with the adults, thus suggesting that early years' pedagogy is relevant to all ages.

The students worked with the kindergarten children each morning and later in the afternoons organised craft-based activities with small groups of different aged children, as requested in the feasibility study. The tutors

Hope One World students takes part in practical activities outside the classroom. SOS Children's Village, Galle, Sri Lanka in 2005.

also met with the mothers of the children and worked on similar craft-based activities in the evenings. During the project both students and tutors remained together. It was well received and the team was asked to return the following year to different SOS villages.

Subsequent workshops

Having evaluated the 2001 project by reflecting on the aims in relation to the needs, it was decided that the 2002 project should involve a more practical approach to the workshops with the teachers and incorporate more active involvement as part of the process in supporting them to speak English. This involved encouraging them to get involved and demonstrate their understanding of new concepts by using and applying the different techniques and ideas, first with each other through practical, fun-based activities that enabled the participants to develop their own confidence. One example of this involved the teachers making their own interpretation of a 'speckled frog' hat so that as a group we were then able to act out the rhyme/song: 'Five little speckled frogs sat on a speckled log....' This allowed the teachers to see how the combination of singing and actions reinforced the new language as well as supporting early mathematical skills. All of the teachers could see that adopting a play-based creative approach led to more effective learning than a formal activity where all of the children were required to do exactly the same activity at the same time. This experience gave the teachers more confidence in their own ability to try out the learning with the children the next day. It also reinforced the initial teaching in the first project and supported the transition from theory to practice. Browne (2001) points out that by speaking children become active learners and develop their own knowledge and understanding.

Although the teachers had a good grasp of English and seemed to have understood the importance of the theory, there was concern that they were wary of making the move from using safe traditional teaching methods to implementing play-based learning experiences which incorporate an element of choice for the children. Their reluctance to incorporate early years' pedagogy was for a variety of reasons. An increased use of learning through play and choice meant that there was less room for direction by the teachers. This meant that the end product was not always what they had planned. Previously examples of art activities included the children being given shapes of fruit drawn or cut out by the teacher: they were then told by them where to stick pre-prepared cut out squares onto their image. Any art work produced by the children always looked the same. As they were used to encouraging the children to work in this way they found it difficult to allow them to produce their own work in the way we expected them to. The use of more speaking and listening-led activities in pairs or small groups such as simple route games, shopping games and big board games all meant that there was less written evidence of formal English lessons, which was hard for them to justify to the directors.

In 2002 one new tutor and one from the previous year to provide continuity went to Sri Lanka. The teacher-workshops took place in a different SOS village with an open invitation to all the teachers from the other villages. Another modification involved taking four students instead of two: they were placed in two different villages in the hope that this would have greater impact. They taught in pairs in the kindergartens for two weeks. The tutors then travelled to another SOS village to give the teachers who had not yet been involved in the project practical workshops. This time we incorporated more speaking into the schedule than previous years and emphasised the importance of talk more which is supported by Tough (1976): this is the essential ingredient within communication and therefore vital in teaching early reading skills. The tutors explained this would involve the teachers in practical activities that required them to use the conversational language that the children would need to use. At the beginning of each workshop session the teachers were asked to evaluate their use of the play-based early reading activities before introducing a new reading related concept. This process was dependant on building positive relationships with the participants. The confidence gained by the teachers through the workshops was important to this. They began to relax and became able to share their concerns and worries which were discussed in sessions. It meant that they began to respond very positively to the new ideas and they began to implement the play-based teaching into their kindergartens.

Student experience

For the students in different SOS villages away from the Hope tutors, the picture was not as positive. Although the whole team kept in touch by phone, the students felt isolated at times and thought the SOS village directors placed unrealistic expectations on them in terms of teaching commitments. They experienced difficulties in planning for larger groups of children, especially with the language barrier which resulted in poor behaviour by the children.

In 2003 the students and tutors stayed together at the same SOS village and worked closely on the same themes as in 2001 and 2002. However, this time the focus was also on the importance of creativity and classroom management. Craft (2001) and Duffy (2006) explain that creativity is now more widely recognised as being crucial in helping children to become more independent, confident and successful learners in all areas of the curriculum. Different teachers attended the workshops and mothers were also encouraged to take part. The directors of the villages asked for parti-cipants to be formally assessed which showed that while the teachers were beginning to understand the need for play-based learning with EAL, the directors still required a more formal approach. Winning the hearts and minds of the managers was crucial to the success of implementing early years' pedagogy. Although the formal request for assessment was not sup-portive of the underlying early years' principles of effective practice, it was important to respect the needs of the partnership: the assessment was therefore modified to incorporate and devise a more creative presentation so that the participants could demonstrate what they had learned and their EAL through small group storytelling or acting or through a song with props and actions. In effect, it was more of a celebration of what the participants had achieved from taking part in the project than an assessment.

The tutors felt that much of the teaching in the kindergarten was now meeting the needs of children in the wider community rather than just the needs of the SOS village children. Talks took place between the project leader and the SOS Director in Sri Lanka who also felt that the project would have more impact if all children in the SOS villages were involved. The focus therefore changed from the kindergarten children whilst they were in school to all children once their school day was over at two o'clock. In preparing the next project there was a continuous flow of communication between the project leader and the SOS director about what the project content overview would involve for both the adults and the children participating.

Project Timetable Overview for 2005 and 2006

Morning
Students
8.30 – 10.30   Prepare practical sessions
Tutors
9.00 – 10.30   Theory workshop sessions
10.30 – 11.00   Break for adult participants
11.00 – 12.30   Tutors lead practical sessions with adults
Afternoon
12.30 – 2.00   LUNCH (mothers welcome kindergarten children back from school)
Students and Tutors
2.00 – 5.30   Afternoon sessions for different ages of children
2.00 – 3.30   Group 1
3.30 – 4.00   Prep for Group 2
4.00 – 5.30   Group 2

Activities for children led by students and supported by tutors (demonstrated theory from morning sessions in practice). Participants from morning sessions by tutors observed and supported.

Roughly 4 Activities each day
Songs, masks, puppets, dough, model making, paper sculpture, language games, stories, songs, parachute games, skipping games and large group games: older children – 14+ use of puppets, story sacks to support younger 3-5 age group in creative activities.

These projects involved the students and tutors working closely not just with the planning of projects but also in terms of implementing and carrying them out. The tutor-led workshops were modified to support the needs of a more diverse set of adults. These included co-workers and non-school educators who worked with the children once they returned from school on sport-related activities. In addition the 'mothers', who looked after up to fifteen children at any one time, and the 'aunts', who were women in the process of being trained as mothers, took part in both groups with varying levels of English. In terms of moving forward the Hope tutors thought it was crucial to involve the directors in the work-shops so that they developed an understanding of why different styles of learning were necessary to support the different needs of the children and how a creative approach through play supports the teaching of EAL. The directors were still keen for a theory-based input to be part of the work-shop sessions. The focus of the workshops therefore was on learning styles and multiple intelligences, looking particularly at the importance of emotional development and effective learning through creativity. May *et al* (2006) clearly identifies that before looking at 'what' is taught, the 'how' needs to be considered: leading one of the tutors on the project to note, 'we don't just pay lip service to the kinaesthetic learners.'

The directors of each SOS village had initially queried how learning styles and creativity would be relevant to the children's learning but their involvement in the interpretative process supported their understanding. The area that required most attention was kinaesthetic learning and teaching through creative, practical activities that promoted EAL. We wanted to continue to find ways to address the findings from the feasibility study which had pointed out that the normal style of teaching involved a more formal 'teacher instructing' approach where children were non-participant learners.

Each of the adult workshops involved an hour of interactive theory followed by practical activities to reinforce the theory. In the afternoon the students and tutors worked with groups of children from the village once they returned from school on fun, practical activities that reflected the morning's teaching. These sessions were scheduled on a rotational basis so that all the different age groups could take part in the project. The children were not used to choice when selecting learning activities or being allowed to talk about their learning or make decisions themselves in relation to their learning: the choice of activities was therefore introduced slowly to the children. By including an element of choice combined with a creative approach, each of the individual learning needs of the children were met. The older children also worked well with the younger three, four and five year-olds, encouraging them to use EAL. As the adult participants worked alongside the non-school educators, having fun, playing games, singing songs, acting out stories and being creative, the children developed their understanding and use of English and the adults began to value the importance of different learning styles and intelligences and the importance of creativity in teaching EAL.

For example, a parachute was used to develop words such as up, down, colours, and instructions while reinforcing auditory and kinaesthetic learning from the morning adult session. The two students reflected on how the session had showed them 'overwhelmingly that to teach English effectively as an additional language, visual, auditory and kinaesthetic learning opportunities need to be available so all children have the opportunity to learn to their full potential.' On another occasion the students reflected how a game they had played developed the children's ability to read English and to transfer their reading into action thus reinforcing their understanding. Having both the English and Singhalese writing was helpful too. This activity reinforced the need for visual, auditory and kinaesthetic learning (VAK), as the children had to read, then go and find things and finally to respond verbally on their return.

Throughout the projects in each village the participants were enthusiastic and willing to be involved. In one village the mothers remarked that they would have benefited from such teaching ten years earlier. One assistant director noted that he could see the links between VAK and the behaviour of the children: he recognised that the non-academic children had been inappropriately taught. However, another director thought that the project would have been more successful had it been longer, perhaps running over three months.

Now that mothers, educators and volunteers are all aware of VAK and different teaching styles, these need to be reinforced in relation to EAL during the next project for a minimum of three weeks. Many of the teachers and educators have left the SOS programme. New teachers and educators need to be included in the project and its focus on EAL through VAK.

Conclusion

Originally teaching English was requested and this is still a priority. However, Rinaldi (2006) points out that effective learning requires an understanding of pedagogy, and the reciprocal relationship between inter-action with others and creativity. In doing so, children are provided with meaningful experiences. Building on the success of workshops that en-courage recognition of this, future programmes will start with the needs of the children and incorporate effective early years' pedagogy. This demands a theoretical understanding and a practical approach to the development of children's emergent literacy and spoken language skills.

5

Design Intervention: Curricular supplementation, public art making, co-operative income generation and cultural exchange

Richard Hooper

The use of Design Interventions in developing countries is an area of increasing interest in the current research climate. In November 2007 the call for papers for the International Association of Societies of Design Research IASDR07 conference included 'supporting development in underdeveloped regions' as one of its emerging topics in the social section. The Brazil design intervention is placed in this wider global context.

Background

This chapter charts the progress of the latest addition to the charity's portfolio: a design intervention with NGOs in Betim, Brazil. It is a response to the proposal put forward by Lessandro Rodrigues and Paula Barros. The two architect graduates came to Hope from the Minas Gerais area of Brazil to study on the Urban Regeneration MA course which they successfully completed in 2003. Knowing about the projects through the Foundation Hour series of talks at Liverpool Hope University, they saw the potential for a project in support of, initially, two Betim NGOs near Belo Horizonte, Salon do Encontre in Betim and Misao Ramacrisna in Bairro Santo Afonso outside Betim. Lessandro had already had contact with these organisations in his capacity as a Town Council member in 2000. Since both organisations have a strong commitment to the arts, it was decided to focus Hope's support for them within Fine Art and Design subjects. Liverpool Hope colleague, Viv Fox, and others travelled to Brazil to explore the viability of these projects and she recommended that the university should support them.

The first cohort of two staff and two students completed projects in the summer of 2003, the first of five years' underwritten commitment from HOW. The following text relates to the Missao Ramacrisna site where, because of its relative remoteness and less integrated civic infrastructure, it was decided to focus the support. Misao is one of a network of NGO's in Brazil whose work complements the state educational system.

The context

Misao operates in parallel with conventional school systems and children attend school in the morning and the NGOs in the afternoon or *vice versa*. Misao in fact operates effectively as a cost centre on behalf of the local authority and pays teachers working at Misao from distributed central funding. Children vary in age from six to sixteen but *alumni* are welcome to attend or contribute thereafter thanks to a welcoming open door policy. The centre opens at 7am and closes at 4pm since it gets dark by 5pm in the winter when our project takes place.

Facilities at Missao have improved dramatically over the five year period of the projects. This is mainly through local support and corporate sponsors, especially the Brazilian Petrobras oil company but is partly due to Hope contributions and donations through sponsorship. The Missao site has two factories, a pasta facility and a wire fence making facility which contribute to their aim for financial self-sufficiency. The site now boasts an impressive performance space and an increasingly well-equipped co-operative crafts area and there are plans for toy making and welding facilities. A vehicle maintenance club is also accommodated on site. Whilst Missao has its origins in the wider eastern Ramacrisna philosophical tradition: it seeks to provide a stable and caring environment in which children can blossom. Missao is situated outside the town of Betim in Santo Afonso, a rural village with a population of five thousand people. There are few employers locally so unemployment is considerable: those who have jobs mainly commute to Betim.

Missao has a twenty strong board of directors who meet three times a year unless additional meetings are needed. It has a Director and two Assistant Directors, all of whom give their time on a voluntary basis, along with twelve or so staff paid via Betim local government, ten administrative staff, five ground/estates staff, three kitchen staff and various ancillary staff. The centre also houses a dentist and an assistant who are also publicly funded. Art and Craft such as ceramics, art, woodwork and weaving run alongside language, numeracy, IT, geography, biology, sport and social development classes. Adults work in productive activities ranging from furniture and toy making, ceramics, weaving and horticulture to a pasta factory and wire fence making. Products are sold either to markets, on-site from display cabinets or at a dedicated showroom at Salon do Encontre. Other sales are by private commission.

Project evolution

Initial impressions were of a well-run and sizeable community facility with a friendly family atmosphere. Although privately run, there was a sense of community ownership and respect for the work there. Access to the site was open and voluntary. There was an interesting balance between education, cooperative industry and pastoral care. The arts were embraced though, as with all teaching areas, resourcing was meagre by European standards. The project brief was open and the Missao Ramacrisna staff were happy for us to initiate any project within reason that would benefit the various groups and age ranges. It was made clear that any materials on site would be freely available to the project. Additional materials would be provided, if needed, by the charity.

Crafts projects prior to our project included the construction of boxes from woven spills. These spills hid the natural qualities of the paper so we suggested the avoidance of the use of this brown colouration. This intervention was the first time we wrestled with issues about cultural taste and our role/right/responsibilities in that context. Post-colonial theory notwithstanding, we all felt we should share our views on this issue. Since the demand for the products in the more cosmopolitan urban markets of Belo Horizonte, Rio de Janeiro and Sao Paulo was growing, we felt this was justified.

The first year was inevitably exploratory in nature although the projects we had planned involving making drawing and modelling studies of natural vegetation proved successful. These were then translated into wall tiles and fired using a handmade *raku* kiln pit. The significance of this was to demonstrate that low-tech processes could be successfully integrated into the production of contemporary domestic products. Upon arrival, site visits indicated the availability of wire used in the fence making factory which was a potential medium for projects. This was subsequently used and a project developed which involved the combination of weaving and the construction of a series of wire spheres. The outcomes became public art and were hung in various locations on the site.

In 2004 the team provided hand tools which were suitable for projects incorporating the wire available on site. Similar work involving found materials was undertaken which was interpreted in wire but with more sophistication as a result of the tools. The motivation for this project was to develop observational skills and sensitivity which had been lacking in the functional and mimetic approaches which had been used before. A further project was initiated making small-scale sculpture and jewellery incorporating lycra which had been donated by a local textile manufacturer. This proved a successful project and some wall pieces were made which were installed in the administrative offices at Missao. Such projects value the use of cheap materials and are consistent with current imperatives to reduce, recycle and reuse. Alongside the classroom work the co-operative was developing and the potential for income generating was seen. HOW staff were asked to develop a range of products which could be made by the co-operative ceramic workers.

In 2005 a ceramic kiln was purchased with the help of money raised by Hope student Anna Kewn in a sponsored swim in the UK. She raised over £500, which paid for a third of the kiln and has enabled fired and glazed ceramics to be produced, giving the cooperative real commercial potential. Further technical capability was achieved by the purchase of industrial sewing machines which have opened up the possibility of producing far more sophisticated products. Other project work with the children showed the potential of newspaper as a sophisticated visual element in jewellery design.

In 2006, staff worked with the co-operative to develop a range of commercial products using clay, fabric and re-cycled paper. The range of products included fashion accessories, clocks and ceramic mugs. Work was undertaken with the co-operative on fashion items which could be manufactured by the workforce while re-cycled newspaper was used to develop a range of table mats and wall clocks, and jewellery was constructed from rolled newsprint. A range of products including fashion accessories, clocks and jewellery were left in Betim for the workforce to develop further products using the skills that were already emerging. The two students worked with the school children on arts and crafts projects using country flags and banners and also introduced Irish dancing. The children experienced their own immersion in another culture as they learnt Irish songs and danced Irish jigs. Dance costumes were constructed which were used in a production which was attended by the whole school.

By 2007 it was clear that certain approaches to working with an overseas partner on a design intervention are mutually beneficial in:

- teaching pupils and teachers
- teaching co-operative management staff and workers
- developing new saleable products
- public art projects
- curriculum and policy development
- purchasing new production capability for school, co-operative or site
- purchasing alternative materials
- showcasing student and staff work
- Shows or donations of inspirational resource material including websites (technology permitting)
- PR via media appearances and simply by being there

Staff or co-operative worker teaching incorporated kiln training, glazing, throwing, surface treatments and slab building. Good learning was achieved which was evident in worker outcomes and responses. A variety of new products were developed such as *cachaca* cups, pestle and mortar sets, candle holders, stands and teapots, which were met with enthusiasm from the hosts. Various lighting possibilities were offered and designs incorporating mirrors were introduced and approved. Public art included mobile and waste material wire design concepts.

The formal integration of performance and movement into the Brazil project took place in 2007. This culminated in a performance piece at the end of the two weeks which demonstrated further possibilities for the expansion of the creative work which had been initiated. The pupils' work was incorporated into collages providing evidence of their achievement. Teaching movement culminated in a performance for a wider audience plus a concert of contemporary music from the UK.

Missao is keen to keep up the momentum achieved in the projects, which have been a rewarding experience for all concerned. The university has been given repeated assurances, written and verbal, that the enterprise is appreciated at Missao and other schools and organisations have asked if similar projects could be set up with them. For all those involved the experience has been highly beneficial, culturally illuminating and wonderfully life-affirming. With clear institutional support, proper management, training, preparation, team selection and communication there is no reason why such projects could not be more widespread. Much is to be gained by all concerned.

6

The evolving role of British students working in an Indian school in Bhimtal

Lynda Richardson and Sue Cronin

Introduction

This chapter explores how a meaningful role for students was negotiated during the 2005 project. This will raise a series of issues relevant to other contexts in which HOW works. The approach adopted provides a blueprint for those facilitating international service learning for students in Higher Education, empowering them to make a worthwhile contribution within a restricted timeframe. A critical incident over the use of inappropriate resources reminds us of how we have to consider issues of sustainability when we work with partners.

Bhimtal – an Indian Project

The partnership with the SOS children's village in Bhimtal is one of two HOW projects in India that does not work with the Tibetan community. The HOW model for the student role in Bhimtal SOS villages up to 2005 had been one of students teaching in the school, providing enrichment as teachers with English as a first language. An understanding of this prior experience was critical to a successful intervention in 2005. Faulkner and Senker (1995) refer to the notion of 'organisational knowledge bases' or how an insider knowledge of a situation is important in improving learning processes and the ability to innovate. HOW uses the local situational knowledge developed by the tutors and students who have visited over previous years to inform the preparations of the new team.

Taking prior experience into account

To some extent each team has a unique experience but there are common useful tips and insights to build on. Reading the evaluations of the student's experiences in 2004 suggested that the student role in the secondary school had been challenging in terms of the subject knowledge required to deliver the curriculum and workload and the work each evening had restricted the students' participation in wider community activities. The 2005 team wanted negotiations to take place with the overseas partners around the student role so they could clarify expectations for the students' teaching and align it to their own experience and strengths.

Tutors were selected for SOS Bhimtal in 2005 to deliver primary and secondary, problem solving-focused, mathematical workshops. The difficulty of communicating with this rural community meant students were not able to plan for their specific input before the project: instead they concentrated on fundraising, preparing generic resources to share on arrival and on researching the SOS children's village and Bhimtal context.

As part of the pre-project training programme in 2005 we expanded it to include a SWOC (strengths, weaknesses, opportunities, constraints) analysis of students' skills and expertise. This additional knowledge base, coupled with the review of evaluations, is what tutors used for negotiations with partners, matching the students to their roles in SOS Bhimtal to maximise their impact. This meant students who were not mathematics specialists would initially team teach to ensure that they remained effective in managing learning within the classroom.

Once in Bhimtal however, 'the primacy of the personal' added to these knowledge-based drivers for change (Chambers, 1997). The personal views and needs of the partners, tutors and students ultimately became the drivers for a radical change of the student role in SOS Bhimtal which emphasised the uniqueness of each team's experience. This framed the perspective, direction and focus of the project.

Primacy of the personal

Initially the primacy of the personal for the students emerged as significant: the research that the students had done about SOS children's villages became a reality when they witnessed the holistic approach of the organisation's stake in the care of orphaned and homeless children. In

70

Bhimtal, the children live in a home with a Hindu mother and family of up to ten children and are educated alongside fee-paying children whose parents pay for attendance at the purpose-built school which is also within the village community. It was understandable that the students wanted to adopt a holistic approach by immersing themselves in each aspect of the children's lives, both at home and at school. The students also recognised that if they worked solely as teachers in the school they diluted the specific contribution they could make to the SOS children's village children because the socially inclusive model of schooling meant that they would also be working alongside the children from the wider community.

The students' drive to be involved in both home and school was validated by the culture and hierarchy of leadership and management in the village. The Director of the village (home and community) provision had parity of status with the Director of the educational, school-based provision. This meant that during our first planning meeting, at which both directors were present, we were able to find out whether it was appropriate for the students to work in the village after school hours. The proposal was welcomed by the Director of the village provision who suggested that the students should participate in communal play and prayer activities as well as in visits to private homes. This further exemplified how the primacy of the personal influenced roles: the Director of the village provision described how interaction in English and being shown examples of productive play would meet needs identified by the mothers who run the homes.

As a result of this convergence of common interests it was agreed that the students would visit the children's homes each evening to model the use of the English language using play-based interactions with the mothers and their families. As both students had identified play-based experience of youth or early years' play provision in their SWOC analyses, this was a mutually appropriate use of their experience.

The importance of personal influences was emphasised again as we toured the school sites prior to our initial planning meeting. The hierarchy of the school provision meant that the primary headteacher reported to the secondary headteacher which meant that decisions were traditionally made from a secondary perspective: the tutors for the previous project had also been from a secondary background. Having discovered that one of the tutors had been a primary headteacher in the UK, the primary headteacher in Bhimtal made a direct request to work with the project team.

A critical incident

Professional development that places teachers in passive roles as consumers of knowledge which is produced elsewhere is clearly inadequate. Little (1993) contrasted the complexity and subtlety of the classroom with the 'low intensity enterprise' of much in-service training for teachers in the developing world that 'communicates a relatively impoverished view of teachers, teaching and teacher development.'

The most successful developmental activities are those where the objectives and design correspond to the priorities of the participants. However, there can be a gap between the desired outcomes and what is achieved. In the SOS Bhimtal project the aims of the school largely corresponded to the aims of the tutors as both groups were keen to see new investigative techniques presented in the mathematics workshops being translated into classroom practice. The issue for the tutors was to ensure that the aims were articulated in terms of successful outcomes in the classroom. The tutors agreed with Franke *et al*'s (1998 p673) view that 'changes in beliefs and practices occur in a mutually interactive process'. To organise effective continuing professional development the change in knowledge and beliefs had to be reinforced by changes in classroom practice.

The importance of the transference of the approaches into the classroom as part of this mutually reinforcing process of change was felt by the tutors to be crucial and brought into sharp focus by a specific incident at one of the first meetings. One of the tutors had been involved in the previous year's project and was keen to ascertain whether any of the strategies or resources were still being used. She enquired about the use of small cubes, known as multilink cubes, brought out by the previous year's team and used in several workshops and were assured that they were in use. The considerable delay in finding them suggested that this was not the case! When they were finally produced the tutor was amused and disappointed to find that the same animal shapes made the previous year were still lying in the box, indicating that the cubes had never reached the hands of inquisitive pupils!

This was a critical moment for the tutors: they needed to make sure that the workshop sessions were directly linked to what happened in the class-rooms. This is consistent with research findings of Alan Peacock of the University of Exeter, School of Education, who has been involved in developing sustainable teacher development in the South based on em-powerment and collaborative engagement. He concluded that workshops alone do not have an impact on professional development for these teachers:

> Teachers may acquire new skills in out-of-school contexts through observation and modelling, but peer coaching and support in situ is essential to sustain changes in practice. Applying these ideas in developing countries has shown that learning new techniques outside the classroom without subsequent classroom support is ineffec-tive in promoting change. (Peacock, 2001, p79)

Many HOW projects have evolved to a more hands-on classroom based intervention which the Bhimtal tutors agreed was a more powerful model for affecting change. The cubes incident was pivotal in determining the approach adopted by the team for the following two weeks.

The emergent student role

It was subsequently discussed and agreed that the students would attend the tutor-led workshops in the afternoons and demonstrate implementa-tion of the techniques in their maths lessons in the primary phase the following morning. The students would be complemented by the tutor from the UK with primary experience, supporting the students to plan lessons for science that enabled learning and teaching through inves-tigative approaches. In both cases the context was taken from the school's syllabus and textbooks to support continuity and relevance, thereby in-creasing the potential for the impact to be more sustainable.

For some of the teachers in Bhimtal, the ability to visualise themselves working in a new way in the classroom was too difficult but watching the students work with their children in their classrooms allowed them to see the possibility of it working for themselves. The effectiveness of this approach was largely dependent on the high calibre of the students in-volved who were resilient practitioners and able to adapt the workshop ideas to the learning environment they found themselves in. The model of the workshop continuum moving from the formal lecture setting for the teachers through to the modelling of the workshops materials in the individual classrooms greatly relied upon the ability of the students.

In working this way the team formed its own tightly-focused learning community, with students and tutors supporting each other in ensuring that the aims of the project were delivered in the workshop and classroom. This had the added advantage of demonstrating collaborative working which was not an apparent feature of the school structure. It was important for the teachers to recognise the tutors' confidence in the abilities of the two very capable students to deliver the messages from the daily workshops. This collaborative style also challenged the normal working pattern of the teachers which seemed to allow little time for professional dialogue between colleagues. The use of the students afforded a new dialogue amongst the teachers who were happy to discuss the practices and activities the students engaged their children in, in the classrooms. It also facilitated a buffer zone with teachers asking the students questions that could be passed on to the tutors and raised in future workshops.

Impact

Ultimately, we must ask whether this organic approach to the negotiation of the student role had a worthwhile and sustainable impact for our partners?

On behalf of the village mothers the Director of the village said that their status had been raised through our involvement in the village. This culminated in their being invited to the formal closing ceremony for the first time. This offers interesting insight into cultural hierarchy and a reminder that the charity's approach to needs-led, open negotiation of roles is important to making culturally appropriate decisions. Both teachers and students noted that the relationships the students developed in the village made a noticeable difference to the participation and confidence of the children during lessons where the students taught or were present. In the school context the students' implementation of the investigative science and maths approaches learned from the tutor workshops resulted in teachers remaining in classes during the lessons, unlike on previous projects. Equally the teachers noted how valuable this had been in enhancing the impact of the suggested pedagogy on the children's engagement and learning.

The students' own accounts of the effect of the experience of working in the village alongside the school was that it had been transformative. The insight into the SOS children's village's holistic approach to home, school and community provision enhanced their sense of social responsibility. Whether the fact that all the students in the team were female meant that the mothers were more relaxed and open to the presence of women can only be surmised.

This chapter presents an overview of what is possible during a brief education intervention in such a context. One event captures the essence of our approach in Bhimtal. During the project the students were asked to teach the primary school choir a song to perform at the closing ceremony. The significance of responding to this request ensured that one of our central values, of partnership underpinned by responsiveness, shared endeavour, openness and service, is lived out. The resulting Hindi version of *You've got a friend* was a highlight of our partnership: there wasn't a dry eye in the house!

7

Putting HIV where it should be – in the curriculum

Lorna Bourke and Alice Bennett

Preamble

The partner communities consider their educational support requirements each year. They may want assistance, for example, to raise
standards in national assessments in mathematics, implement
gifted and talented programmes or to introduce role play to encourage
speaking and listening skills. Malawi requested something different, yet
not surprising given the pandemic that continues unabated. The SOS
Children's Village Primary School in Lilongwe wanted a team to provide
workshops with the overall goal of designing a cross-curriculum HIV/
AIDS education programme. The teachers at the school had attended
workshops organised by other providers before, which had focused on the
causes, prevention and treatment of the disease. It is not unusual for
people attending such workshops to demonstrate signs of shame and embarrassment. Thus consideration of cultural attitudes, values and beliefs
must be built into any workshop programme if complex educational messages relating to health education are to be understood and acted upon.
We have quoted the participants in the education workshops *verbatim* to
exemplify the main points being made. They illustrate the speakers'
understanding of the nature and extent of the barriers to HIV/AIDS education.

Context

Malawi is a developing country situated in land-locked Sub-Saharan Africa. It is rated as one of the world's twelve poorest countries. Partly as a consequence of the need to supplement the payment of debt charges to other countries, which currently run at a deficit of five per cent of GDP, Government resources are diverted from development projects (Booth *et al*, 2006). So Malawi is heavily reliant on donor aid to provide educational, social, medical and emergency relief programmes; it is administered through global charities such as Feed the Children, Save the Children, UNICEF and SOS Children's Villages. The first publicly reported case of HIV was in 1985, when a former Miss Malawi confirmed that she had been diagnosed with the disease. However, any impetus to educate the greater population was squashed by President Banda who ordered any acknowledgement by medical staff and journalists of the extent of the problem to be treated as treason (Booth et al, 2006). By 1994, when the newly-elected democratic government was ready to face the fact that HIV/AIDS was a serious problem and rise to the challenges of directing awareness campaigns, UNICEF Malawi estimated that there were 600,000-800,000 people infected with HIV and by 2000 they expected more than 870,000 children to have been orphaned by AIDS: 48 per cent of children were orphans because one or more of their parents have died as a result of AIDS (UNAIDS, 2000).

Knowledge, attitudes, values and beliefs

HIV/AIDS in Africa is not a single issue: it is heavily bound up with the interplay between poverty, inequality, culture and sexuality. This compounds efforts made to tackle the problem. Although a number of researchers (MacLachlan, Chimombo and Mpemba, 1997; Nyirenda and Jere, 1991) have reported that many people seem to be aware that HIV can be transmitted through promiscuity and unsafe sex and that there is no cure, it is sometimes confused with the traditional disease of *chinyera/ kanyera* (Cook, Ali and Munthali, 1999). In addition, widespread beliefs prevail that HIV/AIDS can be attributed to witchcraft, mosquitoes and a curse from God (Cook *et al*, 1999; Kipp, Kwered and Mpungu, 1992; Wilson, Greenspan and Wilson, 1989). This illustrates the complex nature of the intertwining of diverse modern and traditional beliefs which, according to MacLachlan (1996), are highly resistant to change.

The teachers support the notion that many different views about HIV/AIDS exist in Malawi. This indicates that lack of trust, witchcraft, and beliefs in God are all important to perceptions, as the following quotes suggest:

> [HIV/AIDS] has promoted deceit among medicine practitioners particularly traditional healers who claim to have discovered its medication, *chambe* [a herb preparation].

> HIV creates hatred within communities as some victims suspect that they have been bewitched.

> HIV/AIDS is a plague from God for our immoral behaviour.

> AIDS is another way that teaches people to be honest so sometimes I feel it is good that the disease is there to teach people to obey the creator (God). In turn we must stop sinning to please our creator and then finally it will stop.

> AIDS is not a punishment from God but a disease.

In contrast to initial cases in the UK, transmission of HIV in Malawi is believed to be primarily through heterosexual intercourse. Homosexuality is still illegal in Malawi and it can be challenging for those with previous experience of supporting people infected with HIV/AIDS in the UK to work within a climate of homophobia (Booth *et al*, 2006). In addition, their experience may not be directly relevant because the use of intravenous drugs is not a significant problem in Malawi (MacLachlan *et al*, 1997). What is evident in Malawi is that young girls and women are particularly vulnerable as a consequence of certain cultural practices.

For example, Liomba (1994) reports the implications of the Malawian tradition of sugar daddies: in exchange for school fees and other gifts young girls are forced into having sex with much older men who are often already HIV positive. It also means that young boys are compromised: they are now more likely to have their first sexual experience with an older woman as the younger girls are increasingly engaged in exclusive transactional sex with older men. The teachers we interviewed expressed concern in relation to a number of cultural practices:

> Some other cultural practices should be discouraged such as *kulowa kufa* [a practice where a man slept with a woman whose husband or son had just died, to put to rest the spirit of the deceased]

HIV/Aids awareness in Lilongwe, Malawi.

Some religious groups such as *Apuse Apuse, Mulunga, Afuna Ana* encourage sexual immorality

Religious leaders should discourage initiation ceremonies that involve immoral practices.

Culture may accept the use of condoms unlike religion that looks at it as a way to promote immoral behaviour

Polygamy should be discouraged

Some of the traditional beliefs will be modified and most nations will lose their identity.

This further suggests that volunteers in health education from overseas need to recognise the importance of understanding the cultural context of Malawi and to consider the possibility that a different approach is required for the delivery of the workshops from the approach they use in their own country.

Stigma and discrimination is associated with anyone who falls outside the norm (Goffman, 1968). It is evident, as the quotes from participants in the workshops below indicate, that private thoughts and feelings differ:

When a person has HIV/AIDS people think that she/he is a prostitute

> This disease is attacking the presidents, prime ministers, ministers, doctors, nurses, teachers, and engineers just to mention a few

> HIV/AIDS patients should not be stigmatised or discriminated since there are several ways of contracting the disease and everyone can contract the disease

> Misunderstandings on issues of HIV/AIDS are bringing a lot of stigma

> This disease is reflecting the prophecies of the book of Deuteronomy that 'I will inflict the world with diseases of coughing and thinness to our sins'

However, the collective response to people who are affected is to act in such a way that they become isolated from mainstream society. This is extended to children who are orphaned through AIDS. Cook *et al* (1999) suggest that they are discriminated through the loss of their parents and because even though the Malawian Government signed up for the UN Convention on the Rights of the Child (CRC) in 1991 through which a 'best interests' principle guides programmes for vulnerable children, orphaned children do not have a collective voice nor the resources to participate fully in society. Therefore there are likely to be severe limitations to the attention given to their psycho-social and emotional needs. Although attention to these factors is not only related to how the individual copes with the situation but also to how society responds to it, it is interesting that one study suggests that 55 per cent of their participants did not think that counselling would be worthwhile (MacLachlan *et al*, 1997). This suggests that meeting the emotional needs of the children to assist them to work through the grief process may not be considered a priority.

One of the consequences of the economic situation, coupled with the lack of comprehensive health care services, is that the care of people who are ill is the responsibility of the family. There are limited resources for families to do this. If they are caring for a sick relative then they are unable to work and contribute much needed financial resources to the family. Therefore, it is not uncommon for families to take the decision not to care for family members who they think will die, especially if they are aware that the person has HIV/AIDS as the following quotes illustrate:

When a member of the family gets AIDS the whole family is disturbed entirely

It brings poverty in the family because the sick demand good things to eat such as meat, milk etc

Helpless bereaved family members may end up in poverty.

HIV/AIDS education

The Government sponsored AIDSCOM was an attempt to instigate a widespread HIV/AIDS education programme in primary and secondary schools but Nyirenda and Jere (1991) found that the campaign failed to improve pupils' knowledge of the issue. They suggested that this may have been for a number of reasons, including the lack of a coherent format to the delivery of the material in the series of booklets provided to the pupils in the classroom. Additionally, it appears that for some teachers talking about sex and HIV transmission proved too uncomfortable (Nyirenda and Jere, 1991). Malawi is a religious society encompassing traditional beliefs, Catholicism, Presbyterianism and Islam. A substantial proportion of the donor agencies from western countries have a religious affiliation. In upholding religious beliefs it is usual for abstinence to be preached as the main educational message and for use of condoms to be regarded as sinful (Booth et al, 2006). MacLachlan *et al* (1997) predict that sustainable behaviour change will only occur through a change in pupils' understanding of HIV/AIDS and sexually related behaviours.

However, they suggest that greater understanding is not enough and that teachers could provide an important role in providing opportunities for discussion of the attitudes and beliefs that effect the transformation of knowledge and understanding. Further, Kinsman et al (2001) conclude that extra-curricular school-based HIV/AIDS programmes have their limitations because some key activities such as role play and condoms could only be covered superficially. Therefore, they recommended that school-based education programmes should be integrated into the national curriculum and employ participatory methods of engagement for the pupils. Kinsman *et al* (2001) highlighted that for this to be effective it would require specific training within teacher training colleges. In this context Liverpool Hope University set out to develop a workshop with teachers at the SOS school.

HOW and SOS Children's Villages working in partnership

A number of people, including Booth *et al* (2006), have questioned the lack of cultural sensitivity and historical knowledge of some of those working with donor agencies in Malawi. This is partly due to the nature of postings, which tend to be short-term with not enough opportunity to get to know the communities in which they work. Relationships that foster trust and respect take some time to build up. As Booth *et al* (2006) point out there are few people who have received a western education and therefore the dialogue between charitable organisations and communities is compromised by a lack of understanding of different behavioural characteristics as well as suspicion about the reasons for western involvement. The teachers' quotes below, from the SOS Children's Village, illustrate the shroud of mistrust around HIV/AIDS: They suspect that in order to receive money the government may be exaggerating the scale of the problem.

> I feel the Government and medical personnel hide something on HIV/AIDS because of the donations/funds

> HIV/AIDS has indeed made people rich because when the donors give the country an aid the money is not used for caring those who are affected. Instead the money is used for their own benefit through conducting unnecessary workshops

> There should be openness when delivering HIV/AIDS messages to the members of religious groups

> Some people who work for HIV/AIDS organisations are not committed to their work therefore they are not reaching the required places or areas in time

> The doctors and scientists should tell the truth about HIV/AIDS.

One of the main advantages for Liverpool Hope University is that projects have been conducted within the SOS Children's Village in Lilongwe, Malawi for ten years. This has allowed the charity to build up a relationship based on mutuality and reciprocity. The premise has always been that we all work together to learn from each other, that there is no one right way – just different approaches. It is hoped that the interaction that has taken place over a considerable period of time makes for a trusted relationship and effective workshops. There is a wealth of previous reports and staff experience that to some extent offset the criticisms sometimes leveled at short-term projects. The mission of Liverpool Hope University, whilst recognising its Christian foundation, is to respect all faiths and

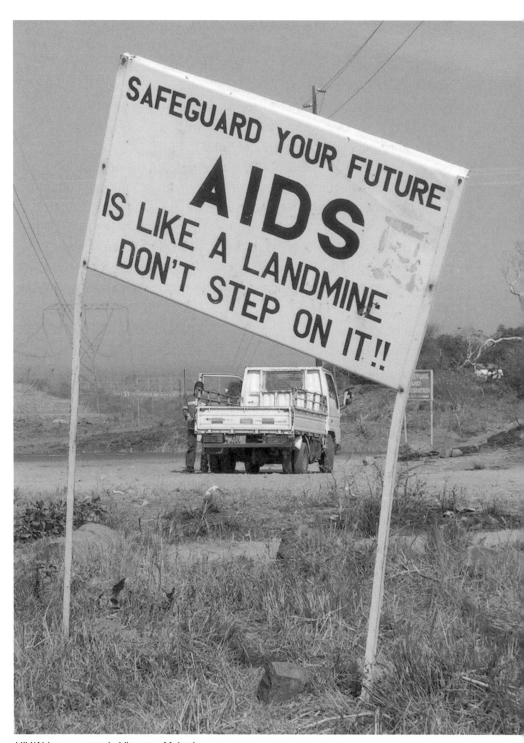

HIV/Aids awareness in Lilongwe, Malawi.

none. In living out the mission staff and students on projects are mindful of this as it is crucial to the degree of sensitivity required to conduct workshops in challenging areas such as HIV/AIDS.

There is evidence to suggest that health education messages that could mean the difference between life and death sometimes go unheeded and are misunderstood due to the attitudes and beliefs of education providers and recipients. Donor agencies are often criticised for their lack of cultural awareness and recognition of the recipients' prior learning experiences in trying to implement education-based workshops. In this context the problems are bi-directional. The teachers in the partner community may hold knowledge, beliefs and attitudes about HIV/AIDS that may be unfamiliar to us and teachers may be unaware of the range of different beliefs and attitudes within their own group and the likely impact this might have on providing a consistent, coherent and effective programme of health education. As the teachers in any school provide the gateway to knowledge and facilitate understanding, it is essential that they are given structured opportunities to develop a deeper and more reflective style to considering challenging programmes of education.

Action research involves a collaborative, problem-solving approach to generate new knowledge. A qualitative research methodology was employed in which the teachers were asked both individually and in focus groups to talk about issues of relevance to education in the area of HIV/AIDS. This included gathering the information the teachers knew about the causes and effects of the virus as well as exploring barriers and solutions to the effective delivery of education on the subject. The teachers were asked to indicate where they thought the responsibility lay for education and the impact of religion, feelings and emotions on the topic area. The responses from the workshops were transcribed after each class and the thematic analyses presented to the teachers in the workshops which followed.

An important aim of the first workshop conducted with the teachers was to create an atmosphere in which they would feel safe to talk honestly about a subject that can be hidden and suppressed. It helped that both people leading the workshops had worked with the participants before. One of the core values of the charity is to minimise the notion of otherness between the partner community and the community in which the project leaders live and work. With this aim the teachers were introduced to the work of Sahir House in Liverpool, UK. This charity supports those living with or affected by HIV/AIDS. Many of the services provided by Sahir House can be directly related to the Reachout programmes delivered by the Medical Centre at SOS. This provided an opportunity for the teachers to develop trust in our expertise on the area. Aspects of current information held by the teachers were clarified where necessary, for example, in relation to sharp objects and needles. It was also possible to inform them about current trends in the UK for the prevention and treatment of HIV/AIDS such as mother to baby transmission, something which has dropped by 10-15 per cent in Malawi in recent years. We were able to work out why some of the practical solutions to problems in the UK were more difficult to implement in Malawi, such as bottle feeding and caesarian births, while others were feasible, such as improving nutrition through locally available and affordable produce. In stressing that there were many possible ways to minimise risks from contracting HIV and assisting those with HIV/AIDS, the sense of hopelessness and helplessness about the virus were visibly reduced.

When we explored the barriers to education on this topic and the possible solutions that could be offered, we found that the teachers had experienced high drop-out rates and poor attendance amongst pupils because of HIV/AIDS. They also recognised that there was stigma and discrimination towards those affected. One of the suggested solutions was to encourage people to go for voluntary counselling and testing (VCT) no matter what they believed their status to be. It was important to clarify the role of the teachers in public health education so that they knew where their responsibilities lay compared with other groups in society. It was also possible that there were contradictions and specific agendas in the messages that were given out by the different groups. The teachers learned to understand how this would lead to conflict in their pupils' minds and the possible consequences of this. Individually, the teachers were asked to write about their own thoughts, feelings and emotions about the issues surrounding HIV/AIDS education. This revealed various themes which were broadly categorised as: prejudice and stigma, collective and personal responsibility, financial and family concerns, mistrust, religion and education.

One technique used in the workshops in response to what arose in discussions was role play. This is an important part of the educational curriculum at the school. It is a technique that is closely aligned to the performance culture in Malawi. The role play game entitled 'Everyone has an HIV status' provided a vehicle through which knowledge, understanding and attitudes towards inclusion and exclusion of people could be examined. The workshop leader explained to the teachers that everyone has an HIV status (i.e. HIV positive, HIV negative, HIV untested) and that each of three designated areas of the room was allocated a different status. Whilst they stood in the middle of the room the teachers were read a series of statements:

- Your CD4 count [a measure of the strength of the immune system taken from a blood sample] is 400

- You are on antibiotics

- Your child is HIV positive

- You are at risk of meningitis

- You are a Muslim

- You are going to die

The workshop leader went onto explain that any of the areas in the room designating HIV status could be correct for all of the statements and initiated the following discussion points:

- A CD4 count of 400 can indicate a weakened immune system in an HIV negative person. Discussion about CD4 count in HIV positive people

- HIV negative people are as likely to be on antibiotics as an HIV positive person. Discussion of likely factors for HIV positive and negative people taking antibiotics

- If a child is HIV positive then it is possible that the male parent would be HIV negative if the female was already infected by another HIV positive person, or had become infected during pregnancy

Exploring the countryside surrounding Lilongwe, Malawi with friends from SOS Children's Village, Lilongwe, Malawi.

- At the time of the workshop programme, there was an outbreak of meningitis in Malawi, so the statement can be true for all three statuses

- There were misconceptions about the effect of Muslim culture and practices on acquiring the virus

- Rather obviously: we are all going to die one day.

Further role play reflected consideration of the implications of the gender imbalance in power in Malawian society. Women have little negotiating power in a relationship and where there is a risk of HIV, this can affect how they can deal with infidelity, HIV testing, and use of condoms.

In the *Negotiating Game*, participants are divided into groups of men and women. The women are sent outside the room and the men remain seated. The men are told that they are now women and they will need to negotiate for their life. They are asked to find three good reasons why they should be given the chance to live. The women are told they have the HIV virus and they must destroy the male participants. Discussion should centre round the fact that so few women in Malawi have this opportunity to bargain. When the men were asked how it felt to be in a weak bargaining position and the women were asked how it felt to wield power over them, the replies were enlightening.

The workshop participants drew attention to the importance of good teaching methods. They had decided that rather than offer HIV/AIDS education through a dedicated life-skills programme, as suggested by Kinsman *et al* (2001), a more effective intervention would be to raise awareness through all subject areas and all levels. The challenge was to create a curriculum that engaged the pupils' interest and was not repetitive. What emerged was an imaginative and creative approach which rested firmly in the hands of the teachers. They had the freedom to decide to use any of the delivery and assessment techniques presented in the sessions, plus their own tried and tested methods. The teachers could incorporate information they thought would enhance their pupils' knowledge and understanding from the range of reference materials made available to them by the project leaders and donated by Sahir House which were published in the main by NAM (National AIDS Manual).

The teachers decided that they would embed information about nutrition, HIV status, incidence and prevalence rates, causes, transmission and prevention, expressing and recognising feelings and family relationships into their curriculum. Importantly, the delivery of the sessions encompassed a wide range of active and participatory teaching methods, including role play, comprehension exercises, games and songs, all designed by the teachers themselves. Interestingly, one of the teachers decided to incorporate the Everyone has an HIV status role play into a PE lesson which was about learning the skills of passing balls in football. Booth *et al* (2006) noted the lack of creativity in collective societies in Malawi. In contrast to this, the programme of learning developed by the teachers at SOS Children's Village, Lilongwe provides evidence that given the opportunity, support and encouragement, there is scope to take a systematic and evaluative approach to realising a different and appropriate way forward for their community.

Workshop evaluation

The aim of the workshops was not to prescribe any pre-designated view on how the teachers dealt with issues relating to HIV/AIDS but to examine the influence of culture on educational messages. It was hoped that this reflective process would help them to draw some conclusions and empower them to determine their way forward in the education of the young people for whom they were responsible. The teachers were asked what their main views were about HIV/AIDS before they delivered the workshops.

Pre-workshop view

Their pre-workshop views were characterised by a sense of fear, helplessness and hopelessness as well as their expectations about the content of the workshop programme which was based on previous knowledge. Below are some of their comments:

We thought an HIV person should just sit and sleep because he/she is useless.

We thought one found with HIV/AIDS would die.

Expectation of being taught about ARVs [antiretroviral drugs that inhibit the ability of HIV to multiply in the body].

Post-workshop view

The concluding comments made by the teachers provide evidence that the outcomes of the programme were being met and showed the specific aspects they were satisfied with.

Satisfied because we have acquired knowledge we did not have.

Sympathy for those affected.

Assisting those affected.

We can go for VCT [voluntary counselling] and testing without hesitation.

We've discovered that HIV/AIDS concern is worldwide and concerned people like Alice [Alice Bennett] help the sick people in the UK.

We enjoyed learning about new ideas on HIV/AIDS, for example, CD4 count, T4 cells [T-lymphocyte blood cell], preparing nutritious drinks, stigma, how to prevent the disease.

It was not necessarily intended that the programme would shift attitudes, as attitude change is known to be difficult. But it did seek to recognise its impact on education. However, it seems from the words of one of the teachers that it may have to some degree succeeded on both accounts.

An HIV person should be treated just like any other person in the society.

The students' experience

Students are an important part of each project and their role is to provide assistance in the classrooms of the SOS Children's Village. When asked about connecting with people and what might prevent this, one student described his anxiety: 'There are certain health aspects when I first found out I was going to Malawi project, the HIV thing and all that. I'm not sure how I felt, even when I left, about that.' When probed for further clarification on how well prepared they were in terms of their knowledge and understanding about HIV, one student responded:

Yeah ... I looked into all that, and what I needed to do. The precautions were there I suppose, and just, you know ... I don't know how you act around it, but I got through it and it's not knowing who's HIV positive, not asking who's HIV positive, it's not making a deal of it all but being conscious as well at the same time.

And they went onto describe what they had learned from the experience: 'There's no problem with contact or things like that. So you can play football, things like that, bouncy balls and all that kind of stuff we were doing. It was just about connecting with people.' This student raises an important point about establishing commonalities in our human experience that go beyond issues of HIV status. They attempted to achieve this by finding ways of developing normal relationships in a situation that is anything but normal. Whilst there are challenges to the delivery of health education regardless of the context, the students further explain how they felt:

The other thing that scared me was their knowledge of HIV/AIDS. For instance, they believe if you sleep with a virgin you will be cured. It's not a rare belief, either, in the villages. Also, education, a woman actually used one of the free condoms supplied by the medical centre in the toilet to wipe her baby's bottom as she didn't know what it was. I can't see how you could put what we know here and transfer it there, if that

Hope One World staff and students visit the market in Area 24, near the SOS Children's Village, Lilongwe, Malawi.

makes sense. I think a whole new different, more simplistic approach would be needed. Also, if you could get the older men of the villages to attend, people in authority. If they attend then I'm sure word would spread and people would be more willing to learn rather than be thought of as 'promiscuous' people learning about the taboo subject of sex.

The future does, unfortunately lie with the children as it's their attitudes and beliefs that will change things. As for sex, they all say 'no sex out of marriage' but from what I heard and saw they're just normal people with normal lusts and thus do normal or abnormal things.

Future developments

The teachers at the primary school at the SOS Children's Village in Lilongwe are still interested in participating in workshops provided by HOW and Liverpool Hope University to gain greater awareness of issues relating to HIV/AIDS. The encouragement given to reflect upon and critically evaluate their needs has led to a need to deliver a more pastoral approach to caring for people with HIV/AIDS. This acknowledgment of collective responsibility is part of the traditional and comparatively less individualistic communities in Malawi. Perhaps, as the views given before and after the workshops indicate, more people can be encouraged through these education programmes which change attitudes, to change their behaviour towards those with HIV/AIDS. The recent request for workshops suggests that they would like information on how to care for and support people living with HIV to live life positively. This is in sharp contrast to previous acts and thoughts of condemnation.

Acknowledgements

We are grateful to Gary Sharp for enabling us to see the role the charity could play in HIV/AIDS education, Sahir House, Liverpool, UK for providing library resources, workshop ideas and inspiration, the teachers of SOS Children's Primary School, Lilongwe, Malawi for sharing their knowledge and understanding so openly and honestly, the students who continued to educate the children whilst their teachers took part in projects; and Phil Bamber who assisted with the student interviews.

PART 3
Learning

8

Preparation for the projects and dissemination of work

Mary Stevenson and Barry Grantham

Many of our university staff, students and colleagues overseas know of the work of HOW only as the finished product which is a staff/student team travelling overseas and carrying out an agreed programme of work with a partner school. In fact the level of organisation, planning, training and monitoring to achieve this visible outcome for up to ten teams each year is huge. We have been involved with the practical management of the charity for many years and offer our experience and ideas to other groups who are embarking on work of a similar nature.

Forming teams

One episode of the BBC television programme *Mission Africa* in 2006 featured a team of British volunteers who had been drawn together to complete a short focused project to build a nature reserve in a remote part of Kenya. The team members had been selected on the basis of their specific skills and expertise. The narrator explained that the volunteers would live and work together in close proximity and often in difficult conditions, and that none of them had met before getting on the plane to Kenya. Our immediate reaction was to question the wisdom of a team embarking upon this work without advance preparation and training. It would not happen on a HOW project.

The core unit is the project team. After the staff and student volunteers are chosen, building up the teams is of prime importance. Teams are not formed by accident but by sustained and deliberate work in sharing common goals and activities and in planning together. The projects are characteristically brief so that it is essential for teams to be able to begin effective work quickly when they come to the partner school. They do not have settling-in time as Gap Year students or VSO volunteers have in other circumstances.

Working within a team offers personal and emotional security as well as a stimulating place to learn and achieve. The safety and security of its volunteers is of paramount importance to us. Supported by the HOW leadership, the project team serve as safe hands supporting the work done by staff and students. We aim to ensure that volunteers are safe and happy whilst on projects and that their work is properly carried out so that the well-being of the host community is in safe hands. The team members work together for some activities and share and discuss ideas where they diverge. Students are always accompanied by tutors in order to assure the quality of their work but the learning is not a one-way process. This is a mutually beneficial way of working when compared to the more usual arrangement where students are sent to a location to work and supervision and support is not so strong.

Yearly cycle of activities

1) Autumn: Debriefing and reporting, awareness-raising, fund-raising and student selection

The cycle of activities associated with the charity follows the academic year. Its starting point is mid to late August, at the same time as the release of 'A' level results, when the university and its staff are actively engaged in recruiting and confirming student places on academic courses for the coming year. Most projects have been completed by this time and although some staff and students will take annual leave, others will be ready to engage in debriefing and reporting procedures. These processes are clearly explained during planning and preparation meetings and require each volunteer to submit detailed personal and professional reports and to attend a debriefing interview with a member of the committee. This is used by HOW to assess the impact of participation in the projects on the Hope volunteers and also on the communities overseas. On the few occasions when personal or professional problems have been experienced by team members the opportunity to attend a confidential debriefing interview has proved invaluable and appropriate support has been provided immediately.

Assessments by team members of the impact of their work with staff and children overseas are compared with official evaluations from the partners abroad who requested the workshops and also from the organisations which raised the funds for the project. With this information the committee can assess the effectiveness of one year's projects and make plans for the next. Our partners abroad are contacted regularly to monitor local situations and to assess priorities for the following year.

In the early autumn all project volunteers are reminded of the need to prepare and submit reports and to attend for interview. They are also reminded to submit examples of images, video clips, sound bites, artefacts and memorabilia which HOW can use for promotional, display and fundraising purposes. It is important for HOW volunteers to recognise the need to select a few significant items from their huge individual collections of images and artefacts, and for each item to be appropriately captioned and referenced. These items are used in display, publicity and fundraising initiatives, in both printed and website promotions and by the university for its printed and online prospectuses.

Freshers' Week: How do I get involved with HOW?

Freshers' Fayre takes place in the week before teaching begins for all students. This is an opportunity for clubs, societies, and student services to promote their activities to new students, many of whom will have read about HOW in the university prospectus and have visited the charity's website. These students are keen to make contact with us at the earliest opportunity and want to get involved; some will take the initiative to contact the committee members listed on the website. An attractive stall at the Freshers' Fayre displays pictures, maps, letters, evaluations, souvenirs and charity information including sponsorship of children, as well as goods for sale and promotional leaflets. Students from the university, many of whom have participated in projects overseas, will be on the stall throughout the day to welcome new arrivals, answer questions, and share experiences. The names, academic courses and contact details of

Hope One World teams celebrate completing their training weekend at Caerdeon, Liverpool Hope University's Outdoor Education Centre in North Wales.

interested students are recorded and each is given a provisional programme of our activities and details of how to get additional information from staff and students on academic programmes who know about HOW or who have participated in projects.

The student group

Many students who express initial interest in HOW are attracted by the possibility of being chosen for an overseas project placement and, although the probability of being selected is high, many interested students will be unable to participate. We do not look for suitable overseas projects for all committed and motivated students who apply and are worthy of selection: it has neither funding nor capacity to operate in this way. Each year the overseas projects supported by us are determined and limited by specific requests from our partners abroad, by our own fundraising and by the financial backing of other charities.

One of the major challenges for students is to maintain interest and support for the work of the charity, including its partners overseas, through a stimulating programme of awareness-raising and fundraising activities throughout the year, without expecting to be selected for a project. Some students are disappointed when they are not selected: they lose interest and turn their attention elsewhere. The officers of the student group have an important role here. They have usually participated in a recent overseas project or supported the work in other ways through volunteering at home. The success of the student group through the year depends largely on the commitment and energy of the student group officers. This is especially true after the date of the announcement of places for overseas projects. The student group plays an important role in inspiring and motivating student support through a wide ranging programme of activities that run alongside the training programme for those participating in overseas projects.

The staff group

HOW is registered with the charities commission and protected and supported by its trustees. It operates independently from but with the support of Liverpool Hope University. The constitution makes references to objects and powers, membership, officers of executive committee, responsibilities, meetings, procedures, and finance. Membership is open to staff at Liverpool Hope University who are committed to furthering the objects of the charity and is extended to include retired members of staff and other known friends and supporters. Whilst students at the university are not eligible for membership of the charity, it has been conventional practice to extend observer status at committee meetings to the president and secretary of the student group.

The Annual General Meeting is held in September. Elections for officers take place and reports from the chair and treasurer about the previous year are tabled. The newly formed committee quickly puts plans in place for the biggest awareness-raising event of the year: HOW Week which is at around the same time as the Christian churches' One World Week in mid-October.

Hope One World Week

During this week a number of activities take place in the university: the aim is to place the charity at centre stage, to raise awareness of and showcase its work, to raise funds and to generate interest and support, includ-

ing attracting potential volunteers. Activities include a major presentation, smaller talks to specific groups of students, displays of photographs
and other publicity, a daily stall selling artefacts from overseas, a raffle and
an auction. At the presentation students who have recently returned from
projects share some of their reflections and experiences with the
audience. For many students this experience of hearing these first-hand
accounts is what attracts them to volunteering for a project. Fundraising
events take place throughout the year, often initiated and organised by
students but HOW week remains the main focus for centrally run activities organised by the committee. Application forms for student and staff
volunteers are available on university campuses and are promoted on
websites during this week.

Student selection for projects
Applying
Towards the end of the autumn term the process of student selection for
overseas projects takes place. Places are open only to current Hope students. There have been one or two instances where a student has had a
second opportunity to take part in a project but Hope students who have
been on a project before may not re-apply. HOW usually attracts around
fifty applicants for about fourteen student places every year and a tight
procedure for selection has evolved. To promote fairness and consistency
the student application form is designed so that all references to the
identity of the applicant are concealed. Application forms are read and
graded blind by at least three committee members according to agreed
criteria. The grades awarded pass directly to the chair of the selection
panel. The selection panel members then meet to decide which applicants can progress to the next stage: approximately half the applicants get
through. All applicants who pass this stage are invited to attend a group
assessment day, and an individual interview. Unsuccessful applicants are
all contacted and offered feedback and are encouraged to contribute to
the work of the charity in other ways, supported by the student group.

Assessment Day
An Assessment day is then arranged and students take part in group
activities which are organised and supervised by HOW training officers.
They are designed to inform students about the work and context of the

projects and to assess students' readiness and suitability to take part. The students are awarded grades according to agreed criteria for their performance.

Interviews

References are followed up. One must be from a course tutor at Liverpool Hope who knows the student well. Individual interviews with a panel of three committee members then take place, usually in the early evening and spread over two or three evenings to avoid clashing with lecture/ teaching time. With approximately 25 students to interview each panel sees five students in one evening at half hour intervals. Interviewees are welcomed and put at ease by members of the Student Group: each of them reads an undertaking which they will be asked to sign if selected. This commits them to comply with the charity's terms and conditions: awareness-raising, fundraising and attendance at a series of evening and weekend team building and training sessions, including a residential weekend in North Wales.

On each of the interview evenings the panel members meet before the students arrive to clarify the questions to be asked and to agree the criteria for grading responses. Consistency is achieved through the use of standard questions across all panels. Student responses are graded according to the agreed criteria.

Feedback

As soon as possible after this process, usually early in December, the committee meets to collate all the grades awarded to applicants during the three stages of the selection process. At this point the number of student places available on projects the following year will be known from ongoing communications with our overseas partners. Examining the grade profiles for each applicant makes the selection of the fourteen successful students relatively easy. It is more difficult to put the students into pairs in readiness for the formation of teams which will eventually deliver specific topics in specific locations across the world. It is important to re-examine each student's background and experience, personality, temperament, strengths and vulnerabilities to make the best possible pairings. The committee decides which projects in which countries the successful students are best suited for.

Pupils from Tibetan Homes Foundation, Mussoorie, Uttaranchal, India meet with young people from Kensington, Liverpool during their visit to Liverpool Hope University in 2005.

In mid-December, successful applicants are contacted and congratulated on their success. At this point they are expected to sign the undertaking which commits them to compliance with HOW's terms and conditions and to attendance at planning and training meetings. The final composition of staff/student teams and decisions about project locations are announced later.

Unsuccessful applicants are contacted at this time and offered feedback. They are encouraged to continue supporting HOW and to target fund-raising activity towards next year's projects.

Committee activity

All these labour intensive activities are run by HOW committee members in their own time. This investment of time is extremely valuable as it is vital for sound decisions to be made. Around this time education leaders at the partner communities abroad are contacted to check and confirm priorities for the following year's workshops. This is especially important for the Tibetan schools in India which close from late December to early March for the winter holidays and for the celebration of the Tibetan New Year.

2) Spring: Staff selection, formation of teams, start of training programme

Old staff partnered with new

Selection of staff is more flexible. Application is open to serving and previous Hope staff and also to interested professional outsiders. Some of our most successful project teams have been led by a tutor pair comprising a Hope tutor and a serving teacher from a local school which is in partnership with Hope. As a major provider of initial teacher education, Liverpool Hope works with around 600 local schools. Staff who have taken part in past projects are encouraged to re-apply because it is beneficial to pair an experienced tutor with a new tutor. As we offer short projects which take place in a context of long-term commitments and arrangements with overseas communities, this strategy helps us to offer continuity.

Needs-led approach

Partner schools overseas will identify their priority areas for training and HOW matches these needs as closely as possible through selection of staff with appropriate academic and professional expertise. Tutors who have not volunteered for a project before complete an application form and attend an individual interview so that committee members can assess their suitability. It is important to draw out the areas of expertise of the staff applicants as this is critical in selecting staff for particular projects. Whilst efforts are made to open up opportunities in this field for a wide range of tutors, the key objective is always to send the strongest teams. HOW remains committed to a needs-led approach to planning and team selection.

This has prompted some challenging debates. HOW is clear that its function is not to be a vehicle for providing enriching professional development for Hope staff, nor to give Hope students a life-enhancing experience: these are positive spin-offs for volunteers who take part in projects and there are benefits and learning at many levels for all involved. HOW supports work to further these benefits but remains clear about its own *raison d'etre*.

105

Student contribution

With some exceptions the academic areas of strength of student volunteers are less important than those of the staff. In student selection criteria there is more emphasis on personality, flexibility, cultural awareness and sensitivity. All students have particular strengths and talents and during the selection process they can explore how these could best be used in the context of a project. The key strength that all will offer is communication in the medium of English. This is widely sought after in the communities with which we work, most of which are in countries where English is the official language of business and of education at secondary level and beyond.

Student volunteers on projects normally work directly with children, both in school and village or home settings. They are not expected to advise teachers or other professionals, although they may participate in workshops run by tutors, and take on a supporting or facilitating role. Nevertheless, their impact upon school communities is significant and their methods of teaching and interacting with the children are observed by local teachers: their work implicitly supports the work of the tutors and makes an impression on teachers and other workers around them.

Virtually all volunteers, staff and students alike, are motivated to become involved with HOW through a desire to make a difference but find that the experience of taking part in a project has a major impact on them professionally, emotionally and intellectually. Early in their recruitment and induction training we encourage them to anticipate the impact of the experience on themselves. They are asked to consider the following quote attributed to Lila Watson, an aboriginal elder from Brisbane, Australia, as she responded to a proposed intervention in her community;

> If you have come to help me you are wasting your time. But if you have come because your liberation is bound up with mine, then let us work together.

Training and development

The training programme for volunteers has evolved over time and is now substantial: it begins before selection is complete as the Assessment Day activities are designed to be opportunities for both learning and assessment. In the spring term, once staff selection has taken place, the first centrally organised event is a meeting at which project teams are assembled and brought together for the first time. After the excitement of finding out who the team members are and where they are going, some important practical details must be addressed. These include synchronising dates, information on passports, visas, international flights, in-country travel and accommodation, travel insurance, inoculations and anti-malaria precautions, food and hygiene, money and credit cards, communications both local and international, personal safety and what to do in an emergency. This can all be overwhelming for some volunteers and needs to be handled with care. HOW has conducted detailed risk assessments for each of its project locations and these documents are distributed and discussed with the volunteers. Every team has a designated leader who will either have visited the location or country before or is familiar with HOW projects in other countries: from this point onwards all planning, coordination and communication is channelled through this person.

This first meeting is quickly followed by a training meeting for all team members and a weekend residential event held at Hope's Outdoor Education Centre, Plas Caerdeon, in Wales. It is vital for all volunteers to appreciate the degree of commitment required and that participation in these training events is of the utmost importance. Volunteers must make the necessary arrangements to attend: the weekend residential event is crucial for team building since the experience takes participants out of their usual environment and enables them to concentrate on planning and preparation without the distractions of home life.

'All those happy faces'
Cultural awareness is a key component of training. For most new student and staff volunteers this is their first experience of travel to a developing country. All must begin to develop an awareness of their own cultural misconceptions and prejudices. They are also introduced to the contested constructs of poverty and development through participation in a series of reflexive activities based around a quote from Anais Nin:

We don't see things as they are: We see things as we are.

The HOW training team addresses these issues in an atmosphere of trust and acceptance: volunteers are encouraged to challenge pre-conceived or over-simplistic ideas about other cultures. For example, a smiling face may be part of the hospitality and greeting traditionally offered to visitors and does not necessarily indicate that the person is content with their life. Practical preparation for work on projects and advice about climate, communications, health and dress form an essential part of training and preparation. This is strengthened by the participation of mentors: staff and students who have recently visited each location and are able to pass on first-hand and up-to-date information for the new volunteers.

Training for effective roles and responsibilities

The training of staff and student volunteers goes beyond the practicalities of ideas for activities, what to bring and resources by inviting volunteers to see themselves as representatives of the wider HOW organisation and as ambassadors of the university. In this way we prepare teams for the role they must play whilst on projects: this is informed by feedback from the team's mentor and others who have visited the location. Issues that arise may include: awareness of the decision making structures at the project, who to contact for what purpose, effective email style and the need for negotiation of appropriate workloads.

3) Summer: Whole team and small team meetings, training continues, practical arrangements

More training

The period immediately after the Easter break is a busy time for everyone: staff and students are preparing for end of course assessments and diaries are full. Nevertheless, the training for summer projects continues and weekday evening meetings are arranged for all staff and student volunteers. Individual teams also meet at mutually convenient times and regular contact is made by telephone and email with our partners overseas. More guidance is given on planning activities and particularly on the gathering of resources. Each project has funds allocated for the purchase of resources and often this means that materials and equipment can be purchased in the UK and taken abroad. Teams are asked to limit funds spent in this way and to be aware of the importance of seeking out local resources in the shops and markets abroad. These resources can be replaced more easily, are more appropriate and their purchase supports the local economy.

'You said you would send me a plane ticket'

Further cultural scenarios are explored in detail: it is important that team members are prepared for immersion in a culture which will include their personal involvement in the lives of people who may be living in difficult circumstances or have suffered traumatic events. Newly-formed friendships and informal conversations can sometimes lead to unrealistic expectations of friends in the host community which can be based on their perception of us as part of a highly affluent society. Volunteers are warned to be careful that their conversations are not misinterpreted as promises and to avoid raising unrealistic expectations of what might be possible. On returning home, responding to an awkward request for money or the opportunity to study in the UK can be much more difficult than dealing with the more visible and obvious beggars and street hawkers selling to tourists.

'My friends and family don't understand'

Most volunteers returning from visiting a developing country for the first time tell us that they were shocked and challenged by some of their experiences, certainly by their first impressions, despite all their preparation. After immersion in the new country and culture for two to three weeks many initially shocking experiences remain uncomfortable to witness but gradually become accepted as normal. The existence and security of the team affords each volunteer opportunities to explore and discuss challenging issues whilst abroad. It can be much harder to deal with the reverse culture shock often experienced on return to the UK.

This can be triggered in many ways including a heightened awareness of personal space and privacy, pace of life, quantity and variety of food, safe water, reliable electricity, fast transport, lifestyle and relationships. Most volunteers return home with photographs, souvenirs, memories and stories and are keen to share them with family and friends at every opportunity. Without the support of fellow team members who have shared every moment of their experiences volunteers quickly realise that family and friends just do not understand and cannot properly appreciate what they are trying to describe. All team members are given advice on preparing to return to life in the UK.

Travel to projects

Detailed travel plans are made for all volunteers: all members of the team travel together from the UK and arrive at the project location together. This journey sometimes involves more than one international flights and could include hotel accommodation and road or rail transport. When several projects are scheduled in the same country and the dates coincide, teams travel together. Return dates can vary and independent travel after projects we have concluded is possible but any such arrangements are discussed and agreed by all team members before departing from the UK. HOW is responsible for all project travel arrangements.

The validity of volunteers' passports is checked and, where necessary, visas applied for. This can sometimes involve submitting letters of invitation and photocopies of the passport of the person abroad who will be responsible for the welfare and safety of the team members. All visa applications are handled by us to eliminate any delays or difficulties with individual team members.

Travel insurance is obtained by HOW with the same company for all volunteers irrespective of whether individuals have their own annual cover, and this insurance includes any period of independent travel: handling claims and dealing with emergencies is easier when all travellers are insured with the same company. The terms and conditions of the policy, exclusion clauses and personal declarations are explained in detail and the Foreign and Commonwealth Office (FCO) website is accessed regularly for travel advice.

HOW carries out risk assessments for each location and produces documents addressing health and safety concerns and likely risks. This covers personal safety and what to do in an emergency and includes details of necessary inoculations against infectious diseases and anti-malaria precautions as advised by FCO and the Liverpool School of Tropical Medicine. All volunteers are required to consult their GP or Travel Clinic to check that they are medically fit to travel and agree to take the required precautions to comply with the charity's terms and conditions. All volunteers sign to say that they have read and understand the terms and conditions of their travel insurance policy, and the risk assessment document relating to their project and that they accept the terms and risks involved.

Emails around the globe, mobile phone dependency

As the date of departure approaches team activity focuses on planning and communications with partners abroad and awareness-raising and fundraising at home. All student volunteers have a fundraising target to meet before their departure and many exceed the minimum required. Advice is offered on currency exchange and the safe use of credit cards abroad and special emphasis and support is placed on responsible and realistic expectations of communicating with other teams and with the UK whilst abroad. Many volunteers do not anticipate the impact of difficult and unreliable communication and may not realise that they will have to adjust to living without phoning, texting or emailing friends and family several times a day. It is vitally important that all team members stay focused on their work whilst on the project and are not distracted by news, good or bad, from home. Families and friends must be made aware of this. However, responsible communications from teams abroad sent back to HOW in the UK are encouraged, and these can be relayed to all members at home and abroad.

Risks and remedies

If a student volunteer needs to pull out at any stage after the formation of a team, the main priority for HOW is its integrity and coherence and its ability to meet the needs of partners abroad. There are no reserves so that if a volunteer has to pull out, he or she is not normally replaced. On rare occasions a student substitution has been made using an experienced volunteer who has visited the project location previously. The situation is different with staff and HOW maintains a human resource bank of experienced staff volunteers, each of whom is available to step in at short notice if required.

Problems can sometimes arise from misunderstandings over agreed dates and travel difficulties and delays. This can result in last minute changes despite careful planning. At worst this can happen just before departure or just after the journey has begun. To prepare for this, we collect all the relevant data for each traveller including personal, medical and dietary information, passport and visa details, insurance, travel and accommodation arrangements and contact details of family at home and agents abroad. Volunteers give permission for copies of this data to be held by the charity, to be lodged with the university for the duration of all the projects and to be sent to our agents abroad. These procedures are vitally important when problems arise.

4) On project

22 seats on one plane

All volunteers have a clear understanding of the arrangements made on their behalf by HOW and what to do if things go wrong. All teams will be collected from the airport on arrival by partners abroad or reliable agents and transported directly to the project location or to safe accommodation followed by internal travel arranged locally. Whenever several teams are travelling to different locations in the same country at the same time, all team members fly out together and are accommodated in the same hotel. The arrangements for the return journey can vary according to opportunities for independent travel but all team members leave the project location together and return to the point of entry before going their separate ways. Each volunteer is responsible for his or her own itinerary from then on and all arrangements are agreed with HOW before departing from the UK.

In the best prepared teams all team members will support each other at all times but the tutors know that they are ultimately responsible for the welfare of the students in their teams up to the point of any independent travel. Before leaving the project tutors negotiate with education leaders abroad about HOW priorities and ideas for future work, without making any commitments at this stage.

5) Between academic sessions: closing the loop – feedback and communications

On returning home team members will usually disperse to relax. Before the new university term begins team and personal reports are written and submitted to HOW. Staff prepare professional reports accounting for scholarly activity and research time for submission to deans and line managers. Financial matters are tidied up and any medical or insurance claims dealt with. Photographs and artefacts for sale are gathered in and all reports are read in preparation for next year's HOW activity.

The next batch of students arrive at the university and the yearly cycle of HOW activity starts all over again ...

9

Teaching on top of the world: The purpose of education in a Tibetan Children's Village

Jean Clarkson

Historical perspective of Tibetan Children Village schools

From its beginning 45 years ago, when Tibetans escaped over the Himalayas and were given refuge in India, the Tibetan Children's Village (TCV) has become a thriving, integrated educational community for destitute Tibetan children in exile and others who have escaped. TCV schools have been established in India from Ladakh in the North to Bylakuppe in the South since 1960. The research reported in this chapter was conducted in the highest school in India in Choglamsar, Ladakh. This is a small thriving town six kilometres outside Leh, a prosperous tourist centre for trekkers and climbers which has greatly grown in popularly and size since my first visit ten years ago.

There are now over 15,000 children in schools in India that have a Tibetan curriculum. Tibetan history and geography are taught with Tibetan music and art. They learn the Tibetan language alongside English and Hindi: exams are taken in the Indian system and therefore in English. The Tibetan Cultural Association, chaired by Jetson Pema, the Dalai Lama's sister states:

> All our achievements would not have been possible without the constant blessing and inspiration of His Holiness the Dalai Lama, as well as the unwavering support

and understanding from the people and the Government of India. And of course, we would not have been able to do so much for our children without the continued financial help of so many good friends around the world, especially the SOS Kinderdorf International, the backbone of our financial support (Tibetan Newsletter, 2006)

When the Chinese annexed Tibet in 1959 many Tibetans were forced to flee for their lives. This situation is unchanged and recent influxes of Tibetan children have been absorbed by the sophisticated and established Tibetan education system in exile in India.

The Dalai Lama, in collaboration with Nehru, decided to protect Tibetan culture and ensure the survival of Tibetan Buddhism by educating the children in their own schools using the Tibetan curriculum: Nehru emphasised that the future of Tibetan culture in India was through education and not by using violence to reclaim their country.

Tibetan Children's Villages were thus created, funded by the charity SOS Kinderdorf, a children's charity begun in Austria just after the Second World War to look after orphan children. Children are often sent to Tibetan village schools in India from Tibet at a very early age to ensure that Tibetan culture and Tibetan Buddhism continues. It is a great sacrifice for mothers to send their children to a life of freedom away from their homes so that their Tibetan culture is preserved.

This purpose of this chapter is to discuss the curriculum intentions of the Tibetan Education Authority in exile and contrast this with the education system in the UK.

The principles of education

The principles of education in any society are determined by its economic and political infrastructure: the Tibetan education system is no exception. The education systems of western cultures such as England and the USA are shaped by the aim for individuals to be fully equipped members of a community and contribute to the economic and social welfare of that community (Coulby and Zambeta, 2005). In the UK children are educated to standards which are accredited with recognisable awards that can be exchanged as currency and school success is measured by qualifications and the results of tests. The education system in the UK uses terms and phrases that are borrowed from industry and commerce such as consumers, targets, development plans and clients and performs many essential functions in a sophisticated, democratic society (Chitty, 2002). The form it takes affects every member of society.

Increasingly our definition of knowledge in an educational setting is to contribute to the economic success of the UK. As an indication of the increasing focus on wealth creation as a major purpose of education, Estelle Morris, former Secretary of State for Education, encouraged academics to quit their ivory towers and forge links with industry and commerce to make knowledge count. Therefore education is now seen as a way of developing the country's economic prosperity (Hayes, 2004). The most vivid example of market orientated demands in the UK was the major review of universities commissioned by the Labour Government. Dearing's review (Dearing, 1997) demanded that all undergraduate courses should prove their employability quota and flagged up a new role for universities to produce more 'work ready graduates'. Knowledge and education is promoted as not an end to itself, to create a rounded person, but as a means to an end – in this case to obtain a good job.

As well as the link between wealth creation and education there is the requirement for education to rectify social problems. From childhood obesity to underage sex, schools are called on to solve the problem. There is rarely a government educational initiative without a social angle. The paper *Every child matters* (DfES, 2005) demands that schools take the lead role in child protection and indicates that educational performance is enhanced by reaching targets in social issues such the prevention of bullying as well as reaching educational standards in academic subjects.

As a result of government initiatives the UK education system is caught between the school curriculum and the economic and social needs of society. As a consequence policies have been introduced to centralise and control the curriculum which stress the basics of literacy and numeracy with a renewed emphasis on social skills.

Background review

TCV managers and staff at the university have had many discussions about the purposes of education in both communities and there are frequently many similarities. The workshops, which are requested by TCV teachers, adhere to the educational policies of the Tibetan Education system in exile. Nationalistic narratives in TCV's education policies make

Teachers from the Tibetan Children's Village in Choglamsar, Ladakh, India take part in team building activities during a workshop in 2003.

claims for the Tibetan culture's distinctiveness. According to Coulby (2000), dominant discourses on the cultural supremacy of the nation or culture and the purity of the legacy to the world are features of the common curriculum in many countries. One of the main functions of the TCV education system, in common with other societies, is to create a strong national identity, maybe because Tibetans are refugees in another country and have no homeland of their own. Hobsbawn (1990) reviews the role of education in building national tradition as selectively transmitting official national culture and establishing a national curriculum as a core value in the construction of a national identity, as in the National Curriculum in England.

Jones and Alexiadou (2001) have used the notion of 'travelling education policies' when referring to the work of inter-governmental agencies such as the World Bank, OECD, EU projects such as Tempus Phare that have developed sets of policy themes which seek to reshape national schooling systems and cultures. Their policy agendas interact with existing traditions, ideologies and forms of national organisation but do not redirect the main purposes of education. The workshops we conduct do not challenge the national characteristics of the Tibetan educational system but seek to work with teachers to make learning more effective, share ideas from the educational system in England as well as respect the aims of Tibetan education.

From discussions with Tibetan school managers there is an awareness that education systems worldwide, schools in particular, are conservative social institutions where tradition prevails. Schools everywhere present immense resistance to change and TCV is no exception. The Tibetan government in exile controls the education curriculum and continues to control schooling but it does not control the socialisation of young people in the way it has in the past. My colleague, Dhowa, who participated in this research, observes that young people are changing the way they dress and their way of talking, that boys and girls go to university, often in Delhi, and 'have modern education and they look like foreigners when they come back to their home but their original soul is Tibetan.'

The flow of cultures, symbols and meanings in a globalised system are genuinely uncontrollable by any traditional mechanism of government. Education systems and schools in particular continue to be the most effective mechanism available to contemporary societies for the dissemination of literacy and knowledge. However it is possible, according to Coulby *et al* (2005), that their power is gradually being diminished. This is as true in Tibetan schools as it is in England. Global media has a major influence all children. Children in the small village school in Choglamsar Ladakh have video and their favourite film during my visit was an American film *Home Alone*. The central concept of this film was quite alien in the Tibetan culture, as many children are orphans and independent, spending a great deal of time unsupervised. The convenience of fast food has reached all cultures and children in Ladakh, like children in Liverpool, enjoyed packets of crisps. The tourist industry in Leh ensures that children have a vast array of different western foods to choose from.

Fashion is also universal and the speed of changes of fashion such as the width of trouser bottoms spreads like wild fire through youth culture. All the teachers wore jeans during their weekend activities at the workshops this year and not the tradition Tibetan dress of the *chupa*, worn to teach in the classroom every day. Many teachers listened to popular music: indeed Nawang, one of the teachers, asked me to write down the lyrics of some songs so that she could teach them to her pupils to improve their English. I was requested to teach the words of a song about the destruction of the environment during the workshop. These changes and the spread of globalised cultures and technology are now as influential in shaping the lives of young Tibetan people's identities as the school curriculum. This spread of a globalised culture would have reached the children if they had remained in their homeland of Tibet, although their knowledge of Tibetan culture may have been curtailed.

This investigation into Tibetan education was undertaken because of my long-term relationships with Tibetan teachers in exile in India which were established whilst working with HOW. I wanted to investigate what the Tibetan teachers believed was the purpose of education and their beliefs about what they were teaching in more depth.

I was working alongside four teachers in the TCV primary school who were teaching classes in English. Workshop activities included puppets and drama as well as a hybrid version of the English National Curriculum, the literacy hour, with shared reading and modelled writing. I interviewed my four Tibetan colleagues. The interviews were all interesting and two are reported here.

Nawang Choedon

Nawang is a young teacher with eight years experience of teaching. She was educated in TCV schools in Dharamsala and did her teacher training in Shimla. She did not much like the school in Ladakh and missed her parents who lived in Bylakuppe in Southern India. When I walked with her to her classroom each day and gazed at the Himalayas I remarked how beautiful it was to work on top of the world with this view every day. She replied 'Mountains pah! I'm sick of mountains I want to go where it's green and warm – back to Bylakuppe.'

She believed that as a Tibetan she had a special responsibility to teach Tibetan children and educate them. She said that losing the country of Tibet makes education all the more important and that before the Chinese invasion people in Tibet were self-reliant. Older Tibetans were uneducated so they lost their country because they were ignorant and too trusting. Children therefore needed to be educated. She said that when the Chinese came to Tibet the Tibetans did not know that they were conquering their country: 'they were uneducated and innocent. They played the role of helper to the Chinese and allowed them to invade.'

Nawang believed that it was important to educate children to know about countries other than Tibet so that they would never be innocent and gullible again. 'The purpose of education is to preserve our culture, tell others about it and also to know about other cultures.'

When I asked her about the status of teachers in the Tibetan community she replied that status depends on the person who is the teacher. If they are good teachers and do a good job they will gain respect. She believed that the Tibetan community generally has a high opinion of teachers. This may be as a consequence of education being at the heart of Tibetan government policy. She stated that teachers receive a handsome salary compared to office workers and that her parents were delighted when she became a teacher.

In the interviews I asked the teachers about the role of education in Tibetan culture. Nawang believed that the education of a child is not just for future jobs and for economic reasons.

> It is to make a perfect man. If all Tibetans are educated there will be less destruction. Education does not only mean reading and writing, it is the whole rounded person. DL says we will get back our country through education not with weapons.

Nawang thought that through discussion with China Tibetans might get their country back and she said she would go back to live there if she could.

> In India we get education free for Tibetan children but we cannot get a good job even with good qualification because we are refugees. I have done all my training in Indian universities and colleges and got a good certificate but I will never work in an Indian school and I would like to get good experience.

Teachers from the Tibetan Children's Village in Choglamsar, Ladakh take part in activities outside of the classroom during a workshop in 2003.

Nawang asked whether teaching was possible in England with an Anglo-Indian certificate. Her loyalties were not to India and she could be considered an itinerant now that she had been ousted from her country.

In the interview I asked whether education in Tibetan culture was improving. Nawang believed that it is improving as people are writing more and more about the Tibetan culture. It helps Tibetans to preserve their culture by teaching about it in school. She observed that children learn Tibetan, Hindi and English but they are learning more and more English because of video, tourists to Ladakh and songs and computers in the universal language of English: 'English is better now than before when I started teaching because of the growing number of Europeans in Leh.'

Nawang took an annual trip to Delhi and bought many books in the English language for the school. She considered that the Tibetan children have an educated vision of the world:

> As a teacher in a Tibet community, although I did not witness the invasion I have a duty to tell the children that they are free to have a Tibetan education because their grandparents died walking across the Himalayas to freedom. When I tell the story some children are weeping. Some children not in Ladakh but in Dharamsala have been forced to leave their parents in Tibet to have an education, never to return. I say you have a special responsibility to work in school. People died for your freedom. You must work hard in school to honour this. This is how I discipline the children and motivate them. They take education for granted and I must remind them.

I asked if Nawang could become an Indian citizen: the answer was that if she applied for citizenship she would have to forgo her Tibetan culture and she did not want to do that. She saw her identity as somewhat contradictory. She is loyal to the Dalai Lama's vision but wishes to improve her standing and work in Indian schools or in the UK.

Dhowa Teyli

Dhowa was also in the workshop. A recently qualified young teacher, he was educated in TCV schools and did his training in St. Mary's College, Pune. He decided to become a teacher because of the influence of the teachers in the 3rd , 4th and 5th grades:

> Those teachers were really great. They informed a lot and they taught very well therefore since my childhood days I was totally influenced by these great teachers so naturally my aim is to become a teacher. I have always focused on this. I have dreamt of teaching in school.

Dhowa believed that the status of teachers in TCV was good. He explained that in his society there are not many educated people so that naturally a teacher with qualifications is respected by society: 'A teacher who is trying to do always good is respected by people in our society.'

He believed that his role in the community was to give an education to the children and not only for them to get jobs. He reflected that people provide education for many purposes: to have successful lives and to understand modern education. He considered it an important aim to give a modern education to our 'coming' children. He said that the aim of education is to make our children 'centralised'. I asked him what this meant and he explained that children should become centred and rounded human beings. To become a good member of Tibetan society was a critical aim of the curriculum. Dhowa said that in his opinion Tibetans valued education. Giving a modern education was not restricted to just reading and writing. More important, as His Holiness always stresses, is the value of spiritual education. Religion is part of the curriculum.

> Dhowa: We try to cultivate heart in our students.
>
> JC: How do you make children into good people? What kind of things do you do?
>
> Dhowa: I advise children to be good human beings through discussion and talk about those great people their lives like Tibetan authors and the Dalai Lama.'

Dhowa is aware of the influence of the outside world and of the role played by foreigners:

> We are sponsored by foreigners. Foreigners think Tibetans are very smart people. We try to save our culture. Foreigners like this and sponsor us. They are interested in our culture and are supporting us because we have lost our country to the Chinese. They want our culture to survive.

According to Dhowa, one aim of the Tibetan system is to produce good human beings as well as employment. Dhowa was aware of the social and economic aspects to education, as Chitty's (2002) model suggests: the social aspect of schooling in the Tibetan villages manifests itself in the concept of others before self. Interestingly, the aim of putting others before self is self-fulfilment.

> JC: What does that mean others are more important than self? That's hard.
>
> Dhowa: 'I' is not important. If other people are more important then you are happy.
>
> JC: Can you live like that?
>
> Dhowa: In our school, teaching children to be sharing and trusting is as important as the 'activity' 'I' is not important according to our culture. There is no 'I' at all.
>
> JC: That's different to western culture when 'I' is very important.

Dhowa further reported:

> There are problems in society because of 'I' There may be a clashes with everyone thinking 'I 'is the best. There is no 'I' everyone is 'other'. Others become very important. You think of the whole community including animals. Kill no animal.

Dhowa explained that the curriculum comprises Tibetan culture, history, geography, Tibetan kings, cultures and religion, social statutes and economic systems. Textbooks are published by the Tibetan Association. Dhowa taught about Tibetan writers concerned with mythology and he worked hard to promote Tibetan culture by singing Tibetan songs. He believed that you can run cultures side by side: Tibetan, western, Indian.

Although only twenty five, Dhowa has seen rapid and significant changes in his town of Leh in a growing tourist area and how this has affected the Tibetan culture. He observed that many Tibetans go overseas seeking a better life. He noticed that everything is changing and that Tibetan culture is engaging in and being influenced by India and western cultures. He said that Tibetan culture is getting reshaped every year. He said 'we don't mind the way they interact with other peoples. They have to change when they interact with other peoples but you do not lose the Tibetan in you.' I talked with Dhowa about the future of education in the TCV. Are Tibetan teachers the gatekeepers of the culture? He replied that Tibetans will in the future be highly educated people through modern and traditional Tibetan education:

> We don't want to lose our own culture but also we do not want to miss the modern educational age. We always try to go together shoulder to shoulder. Now we have the style of Indian education but other education systems like America and English have different system and we must try to include this in our advancement.

Dhowa discussed the concept that the Chinese invasion did much to promote Tibetan Buddhism because Tibet might just be a small backward country no one had ever heard of if it has not been invaded. He saw this as a dichotomy as he mused on the benefits of invasion. 'Buddha moves in mysterious ways.'

Policy Documents

Nawang and Dhowa used the national policy to plan their lessons. This is the Tibetan version of the National Curriculum in the UK. The policy of Tibetan Education reflects their status of a community in exile as these extracts illustrate:

2.4 Tibetan people have a responsibility to themselves and to the whole world to preserve and promote their unique wealth of rich culture and traditions, which is of immense value to the entire humanity, at all places, all times and at all circumstances. It must be ensured that this goal is accomplished.

2.5 The long-term goal of Tibetan People is to make entire Tibet, consisting of the three Cholkhas, into a zone of non-violence and peace; to transform Tibetan society into a non-violent society; and to lead other peoples onto the path of non-violence and compassion.

School assembly in dramatic mountainous surroundings at the Tibetan Children's Village in Choglamsar, near Leh, Ladakh, India.

2.6 Tibet is situated on the roof of the world and her treasured natural resources have a close bearing on the well-being of the great Asian continent and the world at large. Therefore, safeguarding of Tibet's natural environment is paramount and must be ensured.

2.7 The political goal of the Tibetan people is to instil in all people of the three Cholkhas the principles of freedom, democracy, rule of law, non-violence, truth and justice. It must be ensured that all Tibetans – young and elderly – properly understand and practice these principles.

2.8 The Tibetan system of economy must also go together with the aforesaid social and cultural principles. Tibetans must therefore abandon the two extremes of the widely spread systems of capitalism and communism; the two extremes of livelihood of affluence

124

and hardship; and dependence on wrong means of livelihood. A system ensuring self-sufficiency and engagement in honest means of livelihood must thus be followed.

2.9 All Tibetans must have access and opportunity, not merely to hold belief by faith, but to actually engage in their profound spiritual traditions through study, contemplation and meditation, thus enabling them to enjoy both the temporary and ultimate whole-some fruits thereof.

These policy goals are clearly reflected in Dhowa and Nawang's philosophy and strong and unwavering belief system which essentially carry out the Dalai Lama's aspirations.

Discussion

When a culture is endangered the people of that culture value it more and attempt to enable it to continue, sometimes against all odds. When the culture is not threatened it is taken for granted. To have a Tibetan education is considered a privilege that was fought for by the parents of the teachers who participated in this research. However, they report that children waste their education and take it for granted because they have forgotten that their grandparents took flight from the Chinese and walked across the Himalaya to India in order to practice Tibetan Buddhism freely. An analogy would be that my own grandparents fought against fascism in the 1930s and 40s and many gave their lives for the freedom to practice democracy and my parents and teachers remind me of this.

There is a special alliance between Liverpool Hope University and the Tibetan community. Staff and students have created an organic connection that links two communities across oceans and mountain ranges. It links an ecumenical university in Liverpool with a Buddhist community in India. It links people ousted from their homeland to people who travel thousands of miles for the privilege of working with them. Yet when people in the same profession share practice the similarities not the differences emerge. It is the common bonds between people, our lives, our values, our children and their future that unites us.

The teachers in our projects report that they are enriched by the experience of working in partnership with tutors from another country and by sharing professional expertise. As Jones and Alexiadou (2001) suggest, 'travelling education policies' do not intend to change the concepts of the system and this is true of the HOW projects. The agenda of the workshops is to interact with existing ideologies and traditions for the benefit of the children's education. Teachers in schools overseas report that they look to the developed world for a democratic model of teaching and learning. The workshop's aim is to increase the engagement of pupils in education and the workshops are seen as an important opportunity to hear native speakers of English.

The long-term commitment and the development of the strong relationship between Liverpool Hope and the teachers and managers in TCV is a significant part of the process. The significant benefit for Liverpool Hope University staff/students through the professional relationships that are developed through partnerships with TCV and the symbiosis that emerges is a critical part of the project work. The study of this relationship and its outcomes is a major motivation to staff at the university. The professional development of staff is validated by workshop activities in TCV. The HOW project demonstrates a commitment to global development without imposing an imperialist culture. The partnership between the people in the projects, both teachers in overseas schools and staff and students from Liverpool Hope University, is a unique part of the project and is a conscientiously egalitarian way of service learning.

10

Personal Accounts

Liz MacGarvey

As an Irish Catholic child in the fifties and early sixties, I grew up thinking about Tibet as a Shangri-la destroyed by the communist and by definition, anti-Catholic regime of China. The Dalai Lama was a great spiritual leader rather like the Pope and both he and our Pope were His Holiness so we were definitely on his side.

In 1993 I was invited by the committee to go to India to work with Tibetans in exile. The Director of Education had requested English workshops in three locations: Dharamsala, Ladakh and Bylakuppe. Now 43 years old, I had a slight and respectful acquaintance with Buddhism but I knew only a little more about Tibetan culture than I had at age ten. However, my background as a former Head of English in a secondary school, a previous post as an English Teacher-Advisor and my current role as a teacher trainer made me a useful candidate for the secondary part of a primary/secondary team. There was no one else of my background available so it was likely that if the interviewing panel thought I measured up I would be on a plane for a ten-week tour of duty starting in late May. The interview process was rigorous. It is a considered better to send no one than to send someone who was ill-suited to the role of project leader. I worked hard before the interview to find out as much as possible about the Tibetan experience and about Tibetan culture. Along the way I learned some things that caused me to re-frame the Shangri-la myth and gave me some insights into but no sympathy for the ruthlessly secular communist Chinese response to a hierarchical and deeply spiritual culture.

Tibetan youngsters enjoy seeing their picture on the digital camera.

There are some strict rules about how HOW operates: you have little choice of who you are paired with on a project and almost as little choice over when you will set off. These factors are dictated by the expressed needs of our partners overseas. We have discussed this procedure at some length over the years but there has been little change to these fundamental ideals. It is easy to see why: experienced colleagues are often paired with those new to the work and subject requests from partners take precedence over lecturers' preferences for locations.

However, on this first occasion both English team members were new to Hope's overseas work, though we had both worked internationally as in-service providers and my primary colleague was a experienced teacher trainer. We kept in regular touch with the Director and the principals of the schools we were to visit and we had several planning meetings before we flew out. We knew that on our first project in TCV Dharamsala we would be working with teachers drawn from at least five different schools, some of whom would lodge with colleagues at the conference centre (Upper TCV) and others would make a daily journey from Lower Dharamsala. There would be colleagues educated to PhD level and others whose training consisted of a year's training after school. An ambitious training programme was to bring all teachers up to the required basic level for primary teaching. It was important for our materials to reflect their varying needs. By the time the departure date arrived, we were squeezing abundant materials past customs with many pleas to them to recognise our status as workers for a charitable organisation.

With the benefit of hindsight, I can warn against the seductive nature of professional development work with communities who have a deep-seated conviction that education represents a future and a route out of poverty for their students and the community as a whole. Tibetan exiles are also a community of teachers and older pupils who recognise the immense benefits of contact with the west and the value of interacting with native English speakers. 'English is a world language; it is a means by which we can tell our story to the world' (Tenzin Wangchuk, aged 15). It is easy to believe that you are doing something worthwhile because the teachers and the young people with whom you work are readier to embrace any new learning than might be the case with a more cynical and less driven English audience. Partners overseas also take for granted that if you have been sent halfway across the world, you must have something useful to offer. 'In addition, we are grateful to you for leaving your family and home behind to come and work with us....' (Teacher's comment on evaluation sheet).

All this can mean that the standards applied to judging professional development work at home are less rigorously applied by our colleagues in schools overseas. They see the journey and our effort and they also have a duty of care to their guests. They are unlikely to offer negative

Tibetan children in a Montessori School at Tibetan Children's Village, Bylakuppe.

evaluations. Working within our own communities it is easy to see when what we offer is hitting or missing the mark but it is not so easy when working with large numbers of teachers in an unfamiliar culture , particularly where respect and deference to teachers is a given. There will be little openly negative criticism if a programme fails to meet the needs of the users and evaluations will be polite. This means that our own ongoing evaluation is essential.

Across the world we work with communities who have suffered injustice, poverty and gross deprivation. The teachers serving these communities are mainly dedicated and highly professional, though not always highly trained. It is crucial for us to offer what is useful in a relatively short time to highly committed colleagues while working in a different cultural framework. This is the pressure of our work on overseas projects.

This anxiety affected our first session with Tibetan colleagues which involved exposition, group work and feedback. There was a lot of creative activity and role-play. Some of what we did was familiar to our colleagues and some was quite new. Over half the group had travelled some distance to attend the workshop which added to the pressure on us to make sure that what we offered was worth their journey.

The first day's activity was warmly received and we quickly formed a bond with the teachers. However, that night I stayed up until dawn in the TCV guesthouse beneath a portrait of HH the Dalai Lama, rewriting some of the materials I had fastidiously prepared back home. I wondered why I had thought that a programme introducing a progressive methodology for teaching creative writing was appropriate for teachers for whom English was a second language. Why hadn't I concentrated on grammar sessions? I was still feverishly thinking through the changes when the Director, Nawang Dorjee, arrived at 7.30 pm to enquire whether we had slept comfortably.

I told him my concerns and a first important lesson was learned: he listened patiently, smiling. He understood my worries about the varying levels of expertise among the teachers and he understood why I wanted to put more emphasis on grammar and that that was fine. I could go ahead with modifications but I must not lose sight of the main purpose:

> We need you to promote creative practices among our teachers. This is a priority. Attachment to text books and to rote learning is not improving students' learning. Please continue as you planned and stop worrying. It will not help your work. Stay focused on what we have asked you to do.

Then, as now, TCV Education knew what it wanted from education development advisors.

Had I been worrying for no reason? No. Listening to teachers' concerns and adapting materials was undoubtedly necessary. But remembering the brief we had been given by a Directorate which had overseen years of teaching development was critical. As in CPD work at home, varying and often conflicting needs are sometimes expressed by teachers as consumers of service learning. Senior leaders and Directors of Study may see

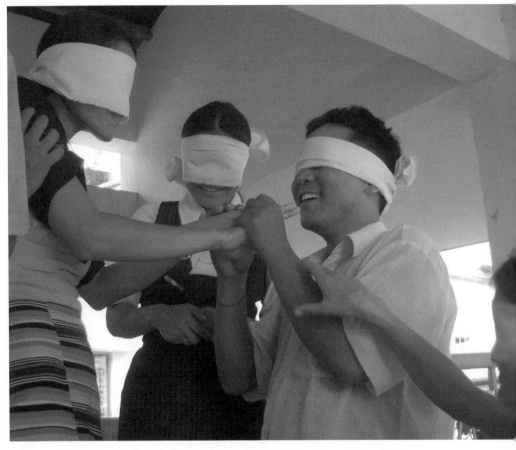

Tibetan teachers take part in team building activities during a Hope One World workshop.

some issues as more important than issues raised by classroom teachers. For us, western educationalists with expertise in our field, our job was to manage competing demands while always remembering that although we might have expertise in our subject area, we are not experts in the culture and community we serve. It is important to keep lines of communication open as early as possible in the programme. This is even more important when working in a large workshop where opportunities for discussion are less likely.

Our programmes last for only about ten days. If anything we do is to be sustainable we have to be mindful of our brief – so that we can stay focused and stop worrying, following Nawang Dorjee's instruction.

On that first workshop my primary colleague and I quickly picked up which techniques from previous workshops had been found useful and what had been quietly dismissed and together we planned a careful evaluative dialogue to establish the best way to secure sustainable progress.

There is also the question of risk in what we provide. The concept of the model lesson is a harmful one in teacher development: it risks suggesting that there is only one way to teach effectively. Involving teachers in seeing and working with the changes you are suggesting is a powerful tool for sustainability. Teachers who hear unfamiliar techniques described want to see them demonstrated and this demands careful preparation and preliminary discussion. The risk is operating in an unfamiliar classroom and culture. A line of teacher observers at the back of the class, keen to observe, certainly sharpens the mind but a thorough discussion of purpose and close collaboration with the class teacher is essential if the lesson is to be more than theatre. From 1993 we established the idea of working alongside teachers in the classroom and whilst economies of scale made the workshop model appropriate then, the future was in the workplace. Even on those early occasions when we only worked directly in the classroom a few times to demonstrate particular strategies or techniques, we were aware of how useful this was to the teachers. The opportunity to interact with native English speakers, whatever the subject area for Tibetan students is invaluable and their response can be overwhelming.

Within the workshops themselves there was a marked division between primary and secondary teachers and mixed sessions were less successful than those in which they worked separately: we were keen to examine these hierarchies with our Tibetan colleagues. Raising this opened up a helpful dialogue which helped to blur the boundaries a little. Nevertheless we accommodated our colleagues' wish to work in their own school sector for most of the sessions. As in the UK, boundaries have become more flexible but training is still more effective when trainers and teachers share their knowledge and experience of particular education stages. In the first workshops we needed to know about the influence of gender and status on teacher participation and sometimes this was hard to establish. The interactions of Tibetan teachers in the workshops showed strong and mutually respectful attitudes but it was much less likely than at home for a new or young teacher to contribute unless prompted.

Several teachers talked about lack of confidence in their proficiency in English: this was particularly marked in Ladakh. Sharp awareness of differing levels of understanding is important, especially where levels of cooperative activity in workshops are so high that the failure of some individuals to understand can easily be missed. In 1993, the process of moving away from teaching through English to teaching in Tibetan and translating subject texts had only recently got underway. In theory the curriculum, from kindergarten through to secondary school, was taught in English. Now it is increasingly taught, especially in the secondary school, in Tibetan. The change has been controversial, especially among English teachers who are concerned that since All India Board exams are currently set in English, students might be disadvantaged by being taught in Tibetan. Debates rage within TCV about the nature of the curriculum and what might be best for young Tibetans facing an uncertain future in a rapidly developing India. Nawang Dorjee said that 'there are even some colleagues who find themselves thinking the unthinkable – that learning Chinese might be as useful to our students' economic futures as learning English is.' There are big issues which are political as well as economic for this community in exile.

As the curriculum in TCV has developed so has the need for precisely targeted interventions. A consequence of professional development and on-going discussion has been a move away from the workshop and towards the workplace. The workshop model which served well for a number of years was felt by our partners to be losing effectiveness. The economies of scale had suggested the workshop model was more useful when schools had relatively large numbers of under-trained staff. As staff in TCV schools became better trained and more confident and training became more widely available from other sources, the special relationship with Hope was in need of re-generation.

In 2001, the Education Directorate of TCV asked if we could move to a new model which would bring Hope tutors into the classroom to work alongside teachers in the classroom.

Tony Edwards

Teaching alongside teachers has become common practice and allows personal interaction between staff from Liverpool Hope University and teachers in the schools of Tibetan exiles. Not having been involved in HOW, the concept 'old model, new model' meant nothing to me: we had been sent to a place which was unknown to us, in a country about which we thought we knew a fair amount: in reality we knew next to nothing. We worked with members of a community whose life experiences were far removed from our own. To compound matters, we were expected to use a new and as yet untried model. The prerequisite for this set of circumstance is to make use of a 'can do' spirit borne out of ignorance rather than dwell on what might go wrong. We were soon on our way.

The Dickyi Larsoe Tibetan settlement at Bylakuppe was established in 1969. It consists of a series of villages constructed on 1800 acres of land which is leased from the Karnataka State government. Most of the original refugees farm smallholdings and supplement their income by running a variety of enterprises including shops and restaurants. Tourists, attracted to the region by the Golden Temple and other monasteries built to accommodate the spiritual needs of the Tibetan Diaspora, are another source of revenue but they are few in number because of the need to obtain a permit before visiting the area.

An SOS Children's Village was built in 1982 between the two largest settlements at Bylakuppe. The village has 32 family houses, each of which is presided over by a resident female warden. In addition there are two single sex hostels, an administration block and healthcare facilities. The educational needs of the largely orphaned community of Tibetan children served by the village are provided in dedicated school buildings. These have either a nursery, primary or secondary focus. The majority of the 1480 pupils enrolled at the school are boarders: they are taught by 139 teachers, most of whom are Tibetan.

Perched on the side of gently sloping hill, the village is entered through an impressive iron-work gate. The site is surprisingly large and is criss-crossed by a series of paths that lead to ever new and changing vistas. They are not roads although they are well-surfaced and the odd car negotiates its way around them. By degrees you become aware of the discreet bungalows, hidden by well-tended gardens which are the main living

Children from the Tibetan Children's Village in Choglamsar, Ladakh, India.

areas. They are squat but solid: there are signs of children everywhere. We arrived early in the monsoon period when everything was green and verdant but it was a constant battle to contend with the elements. Washing lines were draped with rows of clothes which had been hung out by their tiny owners in a vain attempt to get them dry. Training shoes, suspended like strange fruit from any free surface, remained stubbornly waterlogged for days. Only the sound of children punctured the traffic-free quiet of the campus. The sounds of children could be heard from distant classrooms: excited chatter signalled escape from the confines of study. There were also the sounds of the daily rituals associated with communal living: pans were clunked whilst being washed and catechisms were sung, as young voices praised the benefaction of a deity before they had their food.

Preparation for the trip meant anticipating what the needs of both parties in the venture would be. There were only a limited number of clear starting points. The Tibetan group identified the subject areas and discrete parts of the curriculum that they wished to explore, although communication problems meant that some of this information had not been passed on. They also planned an initial series of meetings.

We acquired mainly electronic material on three broad fronts relating to enhancing subject knowledge, teaching and learning resources within each subject area and pedagogy mainly associated with secondary education. A notional programme in which the participating teachers would engage in joint planning exercises was created. This owed more to the need for order rather than having any basis in reality. It was clear that remote planning had limited value. Exploring current practice at Bylakuppe was where the real work would begin. However, one overriding principle shaped how the Hope group prepared for and undertook their task. This was provided by Tsetan Dorjee who won the Best Tibetan Teacher Award in 2006. When asked what characterised Tibetan education he replied that '. . . our students lack independent learning ...' He added that they do not readily go '...beyond what's taught in the classroom...'

The Tibetans were keen to welcome their guests properly and bestow the appropriate blessings upon the event. Seated on an elevated platform and surrounded by dignitaries, we were introduced to their colleagues. In between the formal speeches and ceremony both parties eyed one another nervously. Pale and tired after an exhausting journey and many adventures in between, we were eager not to make any cultural *faux pas* that would compromise relationships. Our nervousness was compounded by knowing that soon we would have to prove our worth. The Bylakuppe teachers followed protocol and showed their senior colleagues and visitors suitable respect: everybody was keen to make a good impression. Despite the formality of the proceedings the benevolence that characterises the Tibetan approach to all strangers was evident throughout.

Practical activities in the primary mathematics classroom, Tibetan Children's Village Dharamsala, India in 1998.

The dignitaries soon left, leaving us to begin the task of forming an effective working partnership. We came from different backgrounds and life experience and were in a strange country and about to use an untried model of working. For both groups there was no rule book to follow: the ideas behind the new model were understood by all parties but there was no substantive practice on which to build or experts to consult. However, professional instincts and a sense of common purpose soon took over.

The formality that characterised the introduction was abandoned and everybody was soon talking about their backgrounds and aspirations for the partnership. The Bylakuppe teachers were surprisingly young and evenly split between male and female. Most were of Tibetan extraction, although a few were Indian nationals. All had undertaken some form of higher education in the subject they taught in the school: some were highly qualified. The women wore traditional dresses and were encouraged by the schools' hierarchy to do so. The majority of the group lived on or near to the campus. They were reserved and deferential. They represented a community of educators who understood their professional needs well. Some were experienced in the traditional model of professional development through workshops because this had been good practice in schools. They were informed about pedagogical issues particularly those associated with the efficacy of child-centred teaching.

The starting point, bearing in mind the words of Tsetan Dorjee, was to see what was already happening in the classroom. This meant that lesson observation of each of the participating teachers needed to take place as soon as possible.

On the first evening we felt a mixture of emotions as we adjusted to strange sights and sounds: exhilaration from our personal and professional journey was tempered by trepidation at the scale of the difficulty facing them. One question resonated: how do you balance all the competing factors without imposing an approach to learning and teaching that is an artificial construct. On a positive note we established a provisional programme with the Bylakuppe teachers through which the quality of the project could be readily gauged as it evolved: the cycle of planning, teaching and evaluation was at its heart.

Stage 1 –   Initial observation of participating teachers

Stage 2 –   Individual feedback

Stage 3 –   Whole team evaluation of needs in the light of Stage 2

Stage 4 –   Lesson planning between individual teachers and the Hope group

Stage 5 –   Further observation

Stage 6 –   Whole team planning of difficult subjects

The risks were many. The individual and collective feedback in stages 2 and 3 had to be honest but undertaken with great sensitivity. Stage 4 offered an important opportunity to mitigate any possible negativity from the feedback. The test of whether the Hope and Bylakuppe groups had become an effective unit would occur at stage 3. Willingness to share experiences at this point would be a sign of the maturity of the team. If they were not then stages 5 and 6 would be jeopardised.

We began lesson observations somewhat cautiously: the teachers had little experience of colleagues watching each other teach, apart from what took place in performance management. The school hierarchy had already expressed an interest in the findings of the observations: this request was politely declined.

The classrooms were traditionally arranged with the teacher's desk at the front: they were poorly lit by small windows that only let in limited amount of light. It was difficult to minimise the impact of the presence of strangers but in the inimitable style of children the world over, pupils soon lost their self-consciousness. The teachers were less comfortable. What was immediately striking was the 'I say, you repeat' routine used throughout all the lessons observed. The cacophony of jumbled sound was striking: children competed to say the answer soonest and in the loudest voice possible. Rather than signalling loss of control it suggested a great energy that was in need of release.

The most immediate conclusion drawn from the observations was the universality of some of the issues facing the Bylakuppe teachers. They had the same difficulty in maintaining focus and the attention of the children as their colleagues in any Liverpool classroom might. Some of the teaching was thoughtful but tended towards a one size fits all model which was best suited to the most able. There was little opportunity for group work and the children were generally asked only closed questions. However, because the school was so orderly it was very easy to forget the scale of the task before them. They had to deal with classes of orphaned pupils of differing ages with varied histories, some very tragic, and teach in a second or possibly a third language. They also had to represent the traditions and values of a community in exile whilst preparing their children for a vastly different world outside.

Instead of being a threat to relationships individual feedback sessions provided an opportunity to dispel any misunderstandings and develop a common sense of focus. The teachers welcomed the chance to talk about their own situation to outsiders and were receptive to the input provided. Informal chat about friends and family also helped to establish a dialogue through which the project could evolve. This process was refined in stage 3 when a list of possible priorities emerged from team discussions. They were

- Separating lessons into discrete but connected parts
- Employing a range of teaching and learning strategies
- Catering for the needs of pupils of all abilities

These were explored in stage 4, the planning exercise, which focused on all or some of the above, depending on individual need.

The Bylakuppe teachers were also keen to see us teach demonstration lessons. On one hand the idea of practicing what we preached was powerful but it belonged more to the previous method of delivery: it ran counter to the spirit of the new model and was fraught with hazards. The Hope group adopted a pragmatic approach: they agreed in principle to give part and whole demonstration lessons but only when the circumstances were right.

The value of lesson observation followed by feedback and a joint planning exercise soon became apparent. In all the classes scrutinised in stage 5 every teacher had made changes to their delivery that resulted in a higher level of pupil participation. In some cases the adjustments were minor: in others a radical transformation had taken place. A science lesson with eleven year-olds who were in their first year being taught entirely in English was outstanding. Pupils exploring different types of motion were marched up and down, thrown balls and given string to swing around their heads so that words such as linear, pendulum and oscillation were demonstrated. They were asked to explain what they had observed. Even those with a poor command of English were persuaded or coerced gently into taking part: it was exhilarating to watch.

Things did not always work well. One colleague found her lesson faltering as pupils who had been encouraged to share ideas struggled to overcome their embarrassment at speaking in public. In the planning exercise the teacher had been persuaded to use this new strategy because she was too polite to raise objections to it. The Hope group did not understand the special challenge that this would present to some of the children. The value the community placed on conformity was very high. It was culturally driven and underpinned by the special circumstances associated with living in exile: it conflicted with expressions of individuality. The demonstration lesson went well but there was an unexpected consequence: in some cases those who had to teach the children immediately afterwards found it difficult to refocus them. The novelty of being taught by someone from another country was not easily countered.

All too soon the gates of the village were disappearing into the distance as the car taking us on the first leg of the journey home bounced its way along the road to Mysore. It was time to reflect. The Bylakuppe teachers had made it clear before we left that the new model was far more effective than the traditional workshop, although much harder for them to participate in. The individualised approach was highly regarded. They now viewed lesson planning in a different light and recognised the value of sharing good practice with each other. However, at this stage it was difficult to estimate the true impact of the project. At its worst it helped to test the model and establish a new rule book with the following advice:

- Be prepared for an exacting intellectual, professional and emotional journey

- Remote planning will be of limited value

- Trust between partners is essential for success

- Planning must be very flexible and driven by clear principles

- Any change in practice has to be organic. It cannot be grafted on

- Special local conditions prevail that will have a bearing on how the project evolves. In India it was important to take into account the pressure on students to perform well in the state examination system when exploring the efficacy of the learning and teaching methods employed in the school.

- Real benefit to all partners would only result from sustained and long term commitment using the same or a similar model

- There is no guarantee of success because of the dynamic and shifting nature of the partnership

Two things summed up the experience. The first was the sight of a young pupil studying a book so intently that she failed to notice that the monsoon rain had found its way into the library and was dripping onto the furniture around her. The second was the almost complete absence of tears amongst the children. We have a lot to learn.

11

HOW to think for a change

Phil Bamber

Everyone thinks about changing the world, no one thinks about changing themselves. Leo Tolstoy (1828-1910)

Overview

This chapter focuses on how the experience of voluntary work in the
developing world changes the lives of the students who take part. It
demonstrates that HOW's work is both informed by and may form
International Service-Learning (ISL) research and policy debate. Present-
ing the narratives of two HOW students and drawing on transformative
learning theory casts light on what students learn and how they learn it.
The discussion that follows draws out implications for practice to support
organisations involved in similar work to exploit the opportunities for
learning that ISL affords. I conclude that while ISL may encourage student
volunteers to think for a change it must incorporate structured support to
transform students' lives and strengthen their resolve and capacity to
sustain action towards a fairer world.

The context

A desire to support the educational development to resource poor communities in developing countries has driven the work of HOW since the
outset when it was known as the Third World Group. HOW's work 'provides a positive instance of globalisation in education working to help
meet the needs of the community, rather than destroying local cultural
values' (Kahn, 1998, p33). This continues to be a primary goal for both

supporters and volunteers. While the charity's purpose statement and publicity material has emphasised 'what we do for them', its strap line, 'Making a Difference, Changing Lives', leaves open the question of whose lives. It appears that participating in a HOW project has transformed the lives of both staff and student volunteers from the UK.

A series of seminars titled 'HOW to think for a change' inspired the HOW internal review process in 2006/07 that involved over 100 staff and student supporters and stakeholders. This revealed a strong sense that significant learning experienced by HOW staff and students volunteers was insufficiently understood, acknowledged and developed in its current work. That HOW's ongoing work was underpinned by the reciprocal nature of ongoing relationships with partners overseas should be recognised and pursued. The conclusion was that our work should have two main thrusts: whilst continuing to strive to meet the needs of our partners overseas, we must also capitalise on the impact of their overseas experience on the UK volunteers.

This chapter contributes to understanding of the ways HOW's guiding principles can be realised. It sets out how students learn from the skills, knowledge and understanding gained from this experience and helps us to recognise the importance of challenging our learning, and broadening it to include the learning generated by service to others. This raises a number of issues of contemporary concern.

'Voluntourism'
Over the last decade, demands by young people from the North to use their gap year to 'make a difference' overseas has led to the proliferation of volunteering opportunities to resource poor communities in the South. This has been exploited by organisations operating without evaluation of the impact on the communities they seek to serve. The 'voluntourism' industry has been accused of being at best self-serving and at worst providing the students with life enriching experiences at the expense of people living in poverty.

There has been little reflection on how the experience might affect those undertaking this work (Simpson, 2004). Volunteers have not been challenged to consider the complex nature of development work. The desire for all UK youngsters to 'learn about the issues that shape their world' has driven the expansion of opportunities for them to volunteer in developing countries listed in the Department for International Development's: Eliminating world poverty: Making governance work for the poor (DfID, 2006, p115). But since global learning or education about development doesn't automatically result from time spent overseas, regulation of the international volunteering sector in the UK is essential (Development Education Association, 2007a p4).

Organisations that advocate a global perspective within formal and informal education in the UK, such as Oxfam and the Development Education Association, stress the need for learning to inform action for change. Oxfam (1997) describes a global citizen as one who is 'willing to act to make the world a more equitable and sustainable place'. But recent research (Kiely, 2004) shows that developing this element of global citizenship over the longer term is problematic. Drawing on data from interviews and focus groups with North American students following their participation in an ISL exposure in Nicaragua, Kiely found that students who feel committed to act upon a transformed view of the world struggle to translate their ideals into meaningful action.

In his study, Kiely (2004 p7) suggests that '....returned students feel compelled to hide their 'true colours' and blend in as a defensive mechanism to avoid being chastised for having 'radical views'. However their defensive conformity leaves them frustrated, 'like a chameleon with a complex'. The Chameleon Complex is discussed in the discourse surrounding adult learning. Looking at the future direction of Global Skills and Lifelong Learning, the Development Education Association (2007b p1) concludes that 'The current challenges are to deepen the level of critical enquiry and move from increased awareness to action for change'. The DEA paper (2007b, p7) points out that 'even when people recognise that specific actions are needed, they often choose not to act'.

Transformative Learning

'I think we all went thinking we were doing something fantastic, and we probably did do something fantastic, but not as much as what ... the effect it had on us.' Angela, Hope One World Participant 2004

A leading research project by Eyler and Giles in the USA into the outcomes of Service-Learning (1999, p133) asserts that 'service-learning practi-

A Hope One World student builds relationships with children in the SOS Children's Village, Lilongwe, Malawi.

tioners tend to come down on the side of transformational learning, supporting education that raises fundamental questions and empowers students to do something about them'. Evidence of the transformative nature of the HOW experience was anecdotal. Drawing on theories of adult learning and the Service-Learning literature, two longitudinal studies (Berg, 2006; Bamber, 2007) investigated the impact of participation in a HOW project on LHU staff and students.

Transformational learning contrasts the potentially transformative nature of adult learning with the formative, socialising and acculturating process of learning in childhood. Mezirow (1991, 2000) describes how transformative learning may lead adults to experience 'perspective transformation', a shifting of their 'world-view':

> Perspective transformation is the process of becoming critically aware of how and who our presuppositions have come to constrain the way we perceive, understand and feel about our world; of reformulating these assumptions to permit a more inclusive, discriminating, permeable and integrative perspective; and of making decisions or otherwise acting on these new understandings. (Mezirow, 1991, p14)

Perspective transformation takes place when our basic assumptions about the world can no longer assimilate a new experience. Confrontation with information that disrupts an individual's world view is the catalyst for change. A perspective change takes place in order to help them make sense of this to 'learn new ways to bring balance back into their lives' (Taylor, 1994, p169). Perspective transformation in the context of an ISL experience may therefore emerge as the unfamiliar helps participants to question the familiar.

Through perspective transformation we question our assumptions and transform our habits of mind (Mezirow, 1991, p20) It is critical reflection on a new insight that brings about a new action. For example, a student's understanding of the nature of social issues at home and overseas, such as begging, may change along with their perception of approaches required to solve related problems. Similarly an immersion in an ISL context can challenge stereotypes and personal values by exposing participants to surprising information that contradicts their previously accepted presuppositions. This may lead to shifts in their attitudes, for example towards beggars, or through a heightened awareness of racial preference, an increased empathy with minority groups.

The allure of transformative learning theory as outlined by Mezirow (1991) ensures that only 30 years later it dominates learning theory in the study of adult education (Taylor, 2000). It served as a framework for investigating perspective transformation amongst HOW staff (Berg 2006) and student volunteers (Bamber, 2007) as well as adult learners in a few similar cases (Taylor, 1994; Kovan and Dirkx, 2003; Kiely, 2004, 2005; Christofi and Thompson, 2007).

A Hope One World student takes part in a traditional dance with pupils at St Peters Catholic Nursery Primary School Ndeaboh, Enugu, Nlgeria

The longitudinal study of eleven HOW students (Bamber, 2007) included case studies in which pre-departure application forms, project journals – where available – and subsequent in-depth interview transcripts were analysed. The findings illustrate the ways in which a student's world view shifts: the nature of changes in attitude. As well as the 'what', this research also identified 'how' participants experience transformational learning during a project. The two narratives that follow offer typical data from these students.

Patrick

Patrick, from a small town in Northern Ireland, was selected to take part in the Malawi project when he was a first year Education Studies student. He spent 3 weeks teaching in the Secondary School in the SOS Children's Village in Lilongwe, Malawi's capital city. The SOS village is home to around 150 orphaned and abandoned children and over 1,000 children come from across the city to learn in the school. The village is also home to Lilongwe Medical Centre, which includes a clinic, children's rehabilitation programme and counselling service.

Patrick was motivated by a desire to do something worthwhile but also a desire to enhance his CV. The experience re-framed Patrick's perceptions of those he found himself living and working with, as he explains:

> All I had ever seen was the news, and of course there were the appeals at school for money for the black babies. While we were in Lilongwe there was a serious water shortage, and the teachers were managing their gardens outside school hours. They were having real difficulties with their crops ... but despite all that, I found a very proud people, who took their circumstances and worked around them. This fundamentally changed my outlook on people in Africa.

Patrick notes that this filtered through to his family and friends at home as if their attitudes were transformed by proxy.

His contribution within the school transformed aspects of his professional knowledge, skills, values and beliefs. Even during such brief immersion overseas he questioned his western-centric outlook with its emphasis on consumerism, materialism and individualism. 'There's more of a community feel, well, in all the villages, that we've been to, than there is here ... people are more tolerant! They take time with each other.' His assumptions about teaching and learning or even the purpose of education were challenged:

> For the first time I actually questioned what education was for. How would completing their Grade 12 exams help these young people function in society? I can honestly say I'd never thought about that before. It has fundamentally shaped my approach in school and in the classroom.

Relationships with individual teachers or community members challenged him as his diary shows; 'These were people I am spending time with, getting to know. It is invaluable.' Exploring these experiences with his tutors was beneficial;

> We'd spend the whole night discussing it ... we hardly ever slept as I remember, because your day would be that full, and then there would be so much to talk about, because you've had your own experiences but then there's three other stories to listen to and that would be meal time... we would all get down, and there were some real funny experiences, thinking back, of talking it through with the team. In particular the meal times were important; that was the best time for reflection for us really.

Patrick described how acutely aware he was of the difficulties in assimilating this transformed outlook in the UK: 'There are things when you come back you can't change... it's such a rush-rush lifestyle over here, it's all about work, work, work... better yourself... how good can you get your life...'. His family however noticed that he was far more tolerant on his return. Patrick recognises his extended citizenship role at both local and global levels. ''I think it's so important to educate people, smashing the silly stereotypes that they have built up, some of the stereotypes that I had.' The HOW experience had brought the actual definition of the problem into question for him: 'We need to educate ourselves, and we need to think, think for a change'.

Patrick felt it was a renewal of faith that led to a new understanding of his role in society:

> You're eighteen, you go off to college, this is great freedom, and you forget about the whole going to church thing. Hope One World has contributed towards spiritual growth for me. And when you're in Africa, you see this kid's going to die of aids, and you see how precious life is, you realise that life's a gift. You've got a huge potential to do things for others. That is my spiritual development, what can be done for others, that my small act may have a wider impact.

On graduation, Patrick enrolled on a Secondary PGCE at LHU, and later took up his first teaching position in a school in partnership with LHU. Patrick has found his career as a teacher a vehicle to draw on his experience and new understanding to make a difference. Patrick is also looking forward to working as a subject mentor with student teachers and feels that his interactions with teachers in the SOS school in Lilongwe have helped prepare him for this.

Jane

Jane lived at home during her college years and as an undergraduate. Her journal provides an insight into her HOW experience in the Tibetan Children's Village in Ladakh, northern India, the most remote and least developed of all the Tibetan communities in exile. It was the first time she had travelled outside of Merseyside: 'I have been away now for four weeks. I always thought I'd never be able to really leave home or go away. I feel like I fit in here more than I do at home'.

This SOS village was established in 1975 and has a number of facilities including homes for the children and a school providing classes from pre-school through to grade ten. Jane worked in the school and lived alongside the children in one of the twenty homes and was accompanied by Hope tutors for only two out of the six weeks of her stay. Jane identifies a number of incidents during her immersion in this community that had a significant impact on her: washing in cold water at the stand pump behind the house, eating with the home mother and children and joining in with prayer.

Jane's approach to her service was transformed; rather than seeing teachers as recipients of aid she became aware of the reciprocal nature of interactions:

> We soon realised that the approach 'this is how you should do it' was totally inappropriate. When we were marking the books we sat in the staff room with the class teachers and had a look at the work and discussed it, we tried to involve them as much as we could and we all learnt a great deal.

This challenged Jane to reconsider what she could contribute. She questioned the use of resources not sourced locally: 'I feel as though it's 'Look what we've got', and you can put it on show and that will surely only make people feel inadequate.' She also reflected on the sustainability of her input and the dangers of raising expectations: 'The village children kept coming round to the house and asking for things. I knew this was because the students before had come and given all the children presents and stickers. I actually wanted to sit and talk to them.'

As well as teaching children in school, Jane supported the Liverpool Hope tutors with professional development workshops for local teachers. 'I could soon see that I was imitating the way they talked to the other teachers and senior managers in the village. They were very effective in getting their message across and making things happen.'

She describes her experience as 'liberating' and a 'journey of self discovery' but also how this process of reflection exposed her: 'In that environment I was no longer defined by all the things and people that define me at home. I initially felt like I was stripped of the things that make me who I am. It was extremely formative' Jane has returned to India on a number of occasions with members of her family.

> For the next few years I was never truly happy being here in the UK and always wanted to be there. I'm always at peace there ... when we fly in, as soon as we get over those mountains, it's like I've come home. I think it is contentment in what you're going to do. It feels like I was born to do that type of work.

Jane and her family have since campaigned on behalf of people with whom she had built up relationships. 'We are always aware of the Tibetan cause, always reading up, keeping in touch. We have demonstrated for the Tibetan cause.'

What can we learn from these accounts?

The narratives of Patrick and Jane illustrate both the types of world view shifts experienced by HOW student volunteers and the ways in which these transformations occur. Furthermore, this empirical data exemplifies how students' critical awareness informs different dimensions of their lives on their return to the UK. The following discussion considers the challenges this raises and implications for practice.

What students learn

■ Transformation of professional perspective

Research (Bamber, 2007) shows that HOW students experience changes of attitude in at least one of the six dimensions identified by Kiely (2004, p11): political, cultural, moral, intellectual, personal or spiritual. Evidence has also been found of an additional transforming form: transformation of a professional perspective. Both Jane and Patrick identify this as significant, suggesting Kiely's framework does not adequately explain perspective transformation within the context of HOW activity.

■ **Students often confirm rather than challenge what they already know**

There is evidence that students do not reformulate 'assumptions to permit a more inclusive, discriminating, permeable and integrative perspective' (Mezirow, 1991, p14). ISL students demonstrate a predisposition to resist challenges to their underlying assumptions. This can be seen in their approaches to poverty and development. One student described their experience driving in a taxi through Delhi: 'It was exactly as I expected it, there were people lying on the ground by the roadside. They had nothing.' The same student spoke of the satisfaction of giving money to beggars on the streets of Delhi. Their thinking had not moved beyond a traditional charitable perspective. Students must be receptive to different aspects of these new experiences.

■ **Students need opportunities to make further sense of their overseas experience**

The interview transcripts of a number of students refer to the 'poor but happy', 'fantastic', 'happy' people they had met overseas. This suggests they view their interactions overseas as with a homogenous group of people who accept their lot as being poor. It may be that they are unable to articulate anything other than this. Opportunities to challenge false assumptions students still hold or ways to communicate their experiences are necessary. When reflecting upon the impact of their work overseas student responses range from those who believe they have indeed changed the world to those who feel they were able to offer nothing. Students must be supported to reach a balanced assessment of the different ways in which they made a difference.

■ **Evidence of perspective transformation is difficult to isolate**

The fact that Patrick considers the causes of high school drop-out rates in Malawi does not warrant a perspective transformation when it may simply be that he had never even considered this issue before: transformative learning is more powerful than simply the discovery of new knowledge. However, there are indications from the interviews that students struggle to articulate ongoing learning that has taken place, resorting to statements such as 'it's difficult to explain' on occasion. Evidence from friends and family also revealed that students may themselves be unaware of shifts in their world view.

How they learn it

Focused pre-departure student training concerning concepts of poverty, development, colonialism, discovery and encountering cultures have acted as a catalyst for student learning. This is complemented by a Student Volunteer Portfolio, a tool to assist HOW participants to structure their reflection whilst overseas and on their return. Although student learning on a HOW project is often serendipitous and incidental a number of factors can be identified as significant:

■ Relationships with community partners

HOW projects provide multiple opportunities for students to 'connect' (Kiely, 2005, p8) with people and places. Learning takes place through non-reflective modes: celebrating festivals together, shopping in the market, playing basketball with teachers, singing with children and catching a local bus. This challenges Mezirow's assertion that it is rational critical reflection that brings about transformation. HOW students contrast their opportunities to build relationships with community members with their previous experiences travelling overseas:

> Before when I travelled in India I was just travelling, and I was moving around a lot, so you don't get the insight really as I've had now living in the SOS Village for two weeks. You pass through, and you may think 'Oh, it's terrible'. But to actually experience it is something totally different. It's because you're living with them, you're eating their food. If you go on holiday you can pick and choose who you talk to and what you do.

■ The approach of accompanying tutors

Tutors who draw on their previous experience, negotiate opportunities for their students to engage with community members and reflect critically with students embody best practice. This depends upon the tutors' capacity to facilitate this process as well as their own world view stances and approaches to difference, development and poverty.

■ Engagement with the local context in safe hands

Issues specific to the context of individual project locations, such as the impact of the HIV/AIDS epidemic in Malawi and the oppression experienced by Tibetans in their homeland, leave a significant impression on individuals. Time to understand the evolving local context is of paramount importance. HOW and the partner communities provide a safe experience for students who had never before travelled outside of Mersey-side. A trade-off exists between exposing students to the realities of the context in which they are serving and scaffolding their immersion. Some students are prepared to 'live how they live every day' yet others prefer to stay in their safety or comfort zone. The extent to which students underlying assumptions are challenged is dependent on their readiness for change and their open-ness to learning.

Learning and action

The research shows that even for this short term ISL experience, re-entry has an ongoing impact. The narratives allude to the potentially de-stabilising personal forces that can be set in motion both during and following the service experience: some students are unsettled in the short term as they perceive friends and family to be unable to relate to or comprehend their experience, others become frustrated as they struggle to translate their transformative experience into action. These tensions provide evidence that a threshold of learning has been crossed. One HOW student eloquently expresses the challenges that make up the chameleon complex:

> I guess what I really want to be is socially conscious, not particularly just concerning the country I visited but also about the world. Having been there and met people who looked similar to the people on the TV you can relate to it a hell of a lot more. The reality of the television and actually meeting people who look similar to the people on TV ... so you can relate, not only to the people there, but the environment they are living in, you can see outside of the TV, you can see what's left and right of it, even though it's not there, you can imagine, and the background to the people, and it has a bigger impact. Other people haven't had that. I don't think I've acted anymore on that... but that's there, and maybe when I'm in a position to act, and to contribute, in certain situations I'd definitely want to do something... be a bit more pro-active on helping causes such as that... it's just difficult at the moment, not having the flexibility to do that...

Conclusion

This understanding of transformative learning should inform attempts to exploit the opportunities for learning that ISL affords. In supporting students to 'think for a change' we must not do our partners a disservice. HOW partnerships are based on reciprocity, mutual respect, openness and integrity: it must be explicit with partners overseas regarding the nature of these goals for students. Organisations involved in ISL that seek to promote transformational learning must account for the different aspects of the chameleon complex: the difficulties and risks inherent when adults reflect on, question and overturn their fundamental assumptions through participation with such programs in both the immediate and longer term. We must explore in more detail the link between global learning and action; the ways in which new understanding leads to changes in behaviour. Preparation underpinned by social justice pedagogy and a formal critical reflection component overseas elevate the outcomes for student learning towards their transformative potential. A framework of persistent and informed support is required if we are to strengthen our students capacity to sustain action towards a fairer world.

Epilogue

Queen's Anniversary Prize

Involvement in HOW has brought many rewards to the staff and students who have undertaken projects during the last twenty years. National recognition is of special significance and in 1996 Liverpool Hope University applied for and won the Queen's Anniversary Prize for Further and Higher education. The Queen's Anniversary Prize has a place in the national honours system and parallels the coveted prize the Queen's Award to Industry and is awarded for excellence in the universities and colleges of the UK. HOW was described as an 'international programme for a refugee community in India that focused on the key areas of educational practice, maths, English and science.' By 1996, 900 Tibetan teachers had been enabled to enhance their educational practice. The number of Tibetan teachers who have participated in HOW workshops has now exceeded 2000. In 1997, *The Times* described HOW projects 'as some of the most innovative and worthwhile ventures in Higher Education.' The citation for the award leading to the Queen's Anniversary Prize read:

> This is a model of international outreach. The effective innovations that have been developed are transferable to other similar communities abroad and have been made available to other institutions.

After a rigorous selection within the university HOW's Ladakh project was chosen for the Queen's Prize vetting process which had specialists assessing every aspect of its achievement and potential. They were looking for clear evidence of exceptional success from an existing project that had benefited its institution and been of service to the international world.

157

HOW committee along with the Vice Chancellor submitted the bid which was recognised as 'an outstanding example of overseas in-service betokening qualities of enterprise, imagination and brilliance.' Staff and students from HOW, with rectorate and members of the governing body, travelled to London to collect the prize. At Buckingham Palace some of the group met with Her Majesty the Queen and the Duke of Edinburgh during the official presentation of the scroll and the gold medal. Later in the picture gallery the royal party spent time with the Liverpool Hope team and were interested in their work with exiled Tibetan children. They were joined by the Princess Royal, Princess Anne, who had spent time in Ladakh with Save the Children.

Memories of the event are still vivid today. As the ceremonial gold medal was about to be handed to the Vice-Chancellor of Liverpool, someone from Edinburgh University dropped their award. The laughter that erupted dissolved the tensions and as the Vice Chancellor of Liverpool received the medal from the Queen there were wide smiles. The Duke of Edinburgh handed us a blank scroll: the original which was hand-written and signed by the Queen might have been damaged by perspiring hands.

Receiving the Queen's Prize was a great honour and the Princess Royal discussed her own work with the Tibetan children in Ladakh with students from Liverpool with enthusiasm. All cultural barriers were crossed. Our students chatted to the Queen about their experiences in India and how it had changed their lives and broadened their horizons to include both university life in Liverpool and the global perspective of Ladakh.

In the picture gallery, under the Canneletto and the Gainsboroughs, the Royal family showed genuine interest. The Duke of Edinburgh was amused at the efforts of one maths tutor who raised funds through a marathon crossword puzzle. A special event like this which recognised the work that had given so many staff and students so much joy was a bonus. Each project continues to give satisfaction and rewards and connects a community in Liverpool with communities across the world. We hope this book will continue to disseminate our work to other institutions and give a wider recognition to education in the developing world.

Bibliography

Africa Progress Panel (2007) Communiqué of 24 April 2007 http://www.africaprogresspanel.org/documents.php

Ajayi-Smith, O. (2005) The role of attitudes in Nigeria's development *National Seminar on Attitude*. National Orientation Agency and Nigerian Television

Aladejana, F. and Aladejana, T. (2005) Leadership in education: the place of Nigerian women *International Studies in Educational Administration*, 33 (2), 69-75

Annette, J. (2005) Community, service learning and higher education in the UK in J. Arthur (ed) *Citizenship and Higher Education: the role of universities in communities and society*. New York: Routledge Falmer

Bamber, P. (2007) The Impact of student participation in International Service Learning Programs. Paper presented to 2nd International Conference on Education for Sustainable Development, Bournemouth University 10-11 September 2007

Banaji, S. (2001) Indian Education in 2001: an overview *FORUM*, 43(3), 151-152

Berg, D. (2006) Gainers as well as givers. Unpublished dissertation: Liverpool Hope University, UK

Booth, D. Cammack, D. Harrigan, J. Kanyongolo, E. Mataure, M. and Ngwira, N. (2006) *Drivers of change and development in Malawi: Working Paper 261*. London: Overseas Development Institute

Botha, R.J. (2002) The Effects of Education. *Journal for Teaching and Training*, 20(2), 52-73

Bourdieu, P. and Passeron, J.C. (1990) *Reproduction in Education, Society and Culture*. London: Sage

Browne, A. (2001) *Developing Language and Literacy*. London: Paul Chapman.

Carrim, N. (1998) Anti Racism and the 'new' South African Educational Order *Cambridge Journal of Education*, 28, 301-320

Carrim, N. and Soudien, C. (1999) Critical anti Racism in South Africa in S May (ed) *Critical Multiculturalism*. London: Falmer Press

Castells, M. (2000) *The Rise of the Network Society*. London: Blackwell Publishing

Chambers, R. (1997) *Whose Reality Counts? Putting the first last*. London: Intermediate Technology Publications

Chawla-Duggan, R. (2007) Breaking out, breaking through accessing knowledge in a non western overseas educational setting-methodological issues for an outsider *Compare: A journal of comparative education*, 37(21), 85-200

Chitty, C. (2002) *Understanding Schools and Schooling: Key issues in teaching and learning*. London: Routledge Falmer

Christofi, V. and Thompson, C. (2007) You cannot go home again: a phenomenological investigation of returning to sojourn country after studying abroad *Journal of Counselling and Development,* 85, 53-63

Clarkson, G.J. (2005) Reformation of the Macedonia teacher education programme 1999-2001 *Education Research*, 47 (3), 319-351

Cook, P. Ali, S. and Munthali, A. (1999) *Starting from strengths: Community care for orphaned children in Malawi.* Final report submitted to the International Development Research Centre (IDRC)

Coulby, D. (2000) *Beyond the National Curriculum: Curricular Centralism and Cultural Diversity in Europe and the USA.* London: Routledge Falmer

Coulby, D. and Jones, C. (1995) *Postmodernity and European Education Systems.* Stoke on Trent: Trentham

Coulby, D. and Zambetta, E. (2005) *Globalization and Nationalism in Education World Yearbook of Education.* London: Routledge Falmer

Craft, A. (2001) Little c creativity in A. Craft, B. Jeffrey and M. Leibling (eds) *Creativity in Education.* London: Penguin

Cramer, C. (2007) Africa on a roll *Guardian* 24 September 2007

Curtis, A. (2005) Play in different cultures and different childhoods in J. Moyles (ed) *The Excellence of Play* 2nd ed. Buckingham: Open University Press

Dalrymple, W. (2007) *The Last Mughal: The Fall of a Dynasty. Delhi 1857* London Bloomsbury

Davidson, B. (1989) *Modern Africa: a social and political history* 2nd ed. London: Longman

Dearing, R. (1997) *Higher Education in the Learning Society: National committee of inquiry into Higher Education.* London: HMSO

Department of Education (1996) *Curriculum 2005: Specific Outcomes Discussion Document.* Ministerial Committee, Pretotia

DfES (2004) *Putting the world into world-class education: an international strategy for education, skills and children's services.* London: DfES

Department for Education and Skills (2005) *Every Child Matters.* London: HMSO

Development Education Association (2007a) *DEA Response to DfID's Public Consultation Document on Youth Volunteering* http://www.dea.org.uk/news

Development Education Association (2007b) *Global Skills and Lifelong Learning: Future challenges.* London: Development Education Association

Department for International Development (2006) *Eliminating world poverty: Making governance work for the poor White Paper.* London: HMSO

Dewey, J. (1938) *Experience and Education.* New York: Collier Books

Duffy, B. (2006) *Supporting Creativity and Imagination in the Early Years* 2nd ed Berkshire: Open University Press

Dyson, T. Casen, R. and Visaria, L. (2004) *Twenty First Century India: Population, economy, human development and the environment.* New Delhi: Oxford University Press

Education for All (2005) *Global Monitoring Report Literacy for Life Summary.* Paris: United Nations Educational, Scientific and Cultural Organisation Publishing

Ejieh, M. (2005) Students' reason for entering Nigerian primary teacher education and their career plans *Research in Education*, 74, 36-46

Eyler, J. and Giles, D.E. (1999) *Where's the Learning in Service Learning?* San Francisco: Jossey-Bass

Fakier, Y. (1998) *Grappling with Change.* Cape Town and Western Cape Educational Department

Faulkner, W. and Senker, J. (1995) *Knowledge Frontiers: public sector research and industrial innovation in biotechnology engineering ceramics and parallel computing.* Oxford: Clarendon

Franke, M.L. Carpenter, T. Fennema, E. Ansell, E. and Behrend, J. (1998) Understanding teachers self sustaining, generative change in the context of professional development *Teaching and Teacher Education*, 14(1), 67-80

Federal Ministry of Education (2000) *Implementation Guidelines for the Universal Basic Education*. Abuja: Nigerian Federal Government Press

Gardner, H. (1999) *Intelligence Reframed: Multiple Intelligences for the 21st Century*. New York: Basic Books

Garuba, A. (2004) Continuing education: an essential tool for teacher empowerment in an era of universal basic education in Nigeria *International Journal of Lifelong Education*, 23(2), 191-203

Gmelch, G. (1997) Crossing Cultures: Student travel and personal development *International Journal of Intercultural Relations*, 21(4), 475

Goffman, E. (1968) *Stigma*. Hamondsworth: Pelican

Griffiths, I. (1995) *The African Inheritance*. London: Routledge

Grusky, S. (2000) International Service Learning *The American Behavioural Scientist*, 43(5), 858-867

Hammersley, M. and Atkinson, P. (1995) *Ethnography: Principles in Practice*. London: Tavistock Publishers

Hankin, L. and Bignold, W. (2006) Globalisation and Global Education in J. Sharp, S. Ward and L. Hankin (eds) *Education Studies: An issues-based approach*. Exeter: Learning Matters

Hayes, D. (2004) *The Routledge Falmer Guide to Key Debates in Education*. London: Routledge Falmer

Herbert, S. (2006) The challenges of designing and implementing a cross-cultural unit of work *Educational Action Research*, 14(1), 45-64

Hobsbawn, E. (1990) *Nations and Nationalisation since 1780*. Cambridge: Cambridge University Press

Idowu, W. (2005) *Civil society, citizenship and democracy*. Gerddes Africa Research Group on the Democratic, Economic and Social Development of Africa http://www.gerddes.org

Integrated Regional Information Networks UN Office for the Coordination of Humanitarian Affairs (2004) Nigeria: crumbling schools and failing pupils http://www.irinnews.org

Iyamu, E. and Obiunu, J. (2005) Impact of citizenship education on the civic consciousness of Nigerian youth *Journal of Instructional Psychology*, 32(4), 305-310

Iyamu, E. and Obiunu, J. (2006) The dilemma of primary school attendance in Nigeria *Journal of Instructional Psychology*, 32(2), 147-153

Jacoby, B. (1996) *Service Learning and Higher Education: Concepts and practices*. San Francisco: Jossey-Bass

Jansen, J. and Christie, P. (eds) (1999) *Changing Curriculum: Studies of outcomes based education in South Africa*. Cape Town: Juta Academic Publishers

Johnson, A. (1998) Another Dark Place of Learning *Guardian* 2 April 1998

Jones, K. and Alexiadou, N. (2001) The global and the national: reflections on the experience of three European states. Paper presented at the *European Conference on Educational Research*, Lille, France 5-6 September 2001

Joseph, R. (1996) Nigeria: inside the dismal tunnel *Current History*, 95, 601

Joseph, R. (1998) Class, State and Prebendal Politics in Nigeria in P. Lewis (ed) *Africa: dilemmas of development and change*. Boulder: Westview Press

Kahn, P.E. (1998) Continuing professional development for teachers of the Tibetan community in India: a case study of the Ladakh Project. Unpublished document: Liverpool Hope University, UK

Kiely, R. (2004) A chameleon with a complex: searching for transformation in international service learning *Michigan Journal of Community Service Learning*, Spring, 5-20

Kiely, R. (2005) A transformative learning model for service-learning: a longitudinal case study *Michigan Journal of Community Service Learning*, Fall, 5-22

Kinsman, J. Nakiyingi, A. Kamali, A. Carpenter, L. Quigley, M. Pool, R. and Whitworth, J. (2001) Evaluation of a comprehensive school-based AIDS education programme in rural Masaka, Uganda *Health Education Research*, 16(1), 85-100

Kipp, W. Kwered, E.M. and Mpungu, H. (1992) AIDS awareness among students and teachers in primary and secondary schools, Kabarole District, Uganda *Tropical Doctor*, 22, 22-27

Kolb, D. (1984) *Experiential Learning: Experience as the source of learning and development.* Upper Saddle River, N.J: Prentice Hall

Kovan, J. and Dirkx, J. (2003) Being called awake: The role of transformative learning in the lives of environmental activists *Adult Education Quarterly*, 53(2), 99-118

Larbi, G. Adelabu, M. Rose, P. Jawara, D. Nwaorgu, O. and Vyas, S. (2005) *Nigeria: study of non-state providers of basic services.* University of Birmingham

Lawrence, E. (1969) (ed) *Friedrich Froebel and English Education* 2nd ed. London: Routledge and Kegan Paul

Leibschner, J. (1992) *A Child's Work: Freedom and guidance in Froebel's educational theory and practice.* Cambridge: Lutterworth Press

Liomba, G. (1994) *AIDS Statistics.* AIDS Secretariat, Ministry of Health, Government of Malawi, Lilongwe

Little, J.W. (1993) Teachers' professional development in a climate of educational reform *Educational Evaluation and Policy Analysis*, 15(3), 129-151

MacLachlan, M. (1996) From sustainable change to incremental improvement: The psychology of community rehabilitation in S.C. Carr and J.F. Schumaker (eds) *Psychology and the Developing World.* Westport: C T. Greenwood

MacLachlan, M Chimombo, M and Mpemba, N(1997) AIDS education for youth through active learning: A school-based approach from Malawi *International Journal of Educational Development*, 17(1), 41-50

Martin, P. and O'Meara, P. (1995) *Africa* 3rd ed. London: James Currey

Maslow, A. (1943) A Theory of Human Motivation *Psychological Review*, 50, 370-396

May, P. Ashford, E. and Bottle, G. (2006) *Sound Beginnings: Learning and development in the Early Years.* London: Fulton Publishers

Mezirow, J. (1991) *Transformative Dimensions of Adult Learning.* San Francisco: Jossey-Bass

Mezirow, J. (2000) *Learning as transformation.* San Francisco: Jossey-Bass

Moss, S. (2007) Madonna's not our saviour *Guardian* 8 June 2007

Myburgh, J. (2004) Politics in South Africa. *Journal of African Affairs,* 103(411), 318-322

Naidoo, J. (1996) *Racial Integration of Public Schools in South Africa.* Education Policy Unit: University of Natal, Durban

Nayana Tara, S (2007) Indian elementary education at the crossroads: way forward *Education 3-13*, 35(1), 29-45

Nieto, J. (2000) *Language, Culture and Teaching.* NewYork: Longman

Nwaokolo, P. (1998) The status of teachers in Nigeria *The Asaba Educator: Technical and Science Education Journal*, 1(1), 6-15

Nyirenda, D. and Jere, D.R. (1991) An evaluation report for AIDS education materials. Malawi Institute of Education, Domasi

O'Connor, A. (2007) Intellectual Power of India takes hold in the UK *The Times* 23 July 2007

Odia, L. and Omofonmwan, S. (2007) Educational system in Nigeria: problems and prospects *Journal of Social Science*, 14(1), 81-86

Ofoegbu, F. and Nwadiani, M. (2006) Level of perceived stress among lecturers in Nigerian universities *Journal of Instructional Psychology*, 33(1), 66-74

Ogiegbaen, S. and Uwameiye, R. (2005) Analysis of factors influencing negative attitude toward teacher education in Nigeria *Education*, 126(2), 292-303

Onimode, B. (1982) *Imperialism and underdevelopment in Nigeria: the dialectics of mass poverty.* London: Zed Press

Onyeizugbo, E. (2003) Effects of Gender, Age and Education on Assertiveness in a Nigerian Sample *Psychology of Women Quarterly*, 27(1), 12-16

Osaghae, E. (1998) *Crippled giant: Nigeria since independence.* London: Hurst

Osunde, A. and Izevbigie, T. (2006) An assessment of teachers' attitude towards teaching profession in Midwestern Nigeria *Education*, 126(3), 462-467

Oyetunde, T. (2002) Second-language reading: insights from Nigerian primary schools *Reading Teacher*, 55(8), 748-755

OXFAM (1997) *A Curriculum for Global Citizenship.* Oxford: OXFAM

Pandey, S. (2004) *Teacher Education researches in Developing Countries: a review of Indian Studies.* Delhi London

Peacock, A. (2001) Helping teachers to develop competence criteria for evaluating their professional development *International Journal of Educational Development*, 21(1), 79-92

Republic of South Africa (1996) *Constitution of the Republic of South Africa Act 108 of 1996.* Pretoria, Government Printer

Rice, X. (2006) Population explosion threatens to trap Africa in cycle of poverty *Guardian* 25 August 2006

Rinaldi, C. (2006) *In Dialogue with Reggio Emilia: Listening, researching and learning.* London: Routledge

Simpson, K. (2004) Doing Development: The gap year, volunteer tourists and a popular practice of development *Journal of International Development*, 16(5), 681-692

Singh, P. (2000) Effects of a Shared Vision *South African Journal of Education*, 20(2), 108-114

Singh, L C and Malhoura, S P (1991) Research in Teacher Education: a trend report in M.P Buch *Fourth Survey of Research in Education* 11. New Delhi. National Council of Education Research and Training

Sobiechowska, P. and Maisch, M., (2006) Work-based learning: in search of an effective model *Educational Action Research*, 14(2), 267-286

SOS Kinderdorf International (2007) *Nigeria: work in progress* http://www.sos-childrensvillages.org

Soudien, C. (1998) 'We Know Why We're Here' – The Experience of African Children in Coloured Schools in Cape Town *Race, Ethnicity and Education*, 1, 7-29

Squelch, J. (1993) Education for Equality: The challenge to multicultural education in E.I. Dekker and E.M. Lemmer *Critical Issuers in Modern Education*. Durban: Butterworth

Stier, J. (2002) *Internationalisation in higher education: unexplored possibilities and unavoidable challenges* Paper presented at the European Conference on Educational Research, University of Lisbon, 11-14 September 2002.

Stock, R. (1995) *Africa south of the Sahara: a geographical interpretation.* New York: Guilford Press

Stromquist, N.P. and Monkman, K. (2000) *Globalisation and Education: integration and contestation across cultures.* Lanham: Rowman and Littlefield

Taylor, E.W. (1994) Intercultural competency: A transformative learning process *Adult Education Quarterly.* 44(3), 154-174

Teachers' Registration Council of Nigeria (2005) *Teaching for Excellence.* http://www.trcn.gov.ng/index.php

Tough, J. (1976) *Listening to Children Talking; a Guide to the Appraisal of Children's Use of Language.* Cardiff: Ward Lock Educational in association with Drake Educational Associates

Transparency International Corruption Perceptions Index (2004) http://ww1.transparency.org/cpi/2004

Uchendu, P. (1993) *Perspectives in Nigerian Education.* Enugu: Fourth Dimension Publishing

UNAIDS (2006) UNAIDS report on the global AIDS epidemic. Annex 2: HIV/AIDS estimates and data, 2005

United Nations International Children's Emergency Fund (2005) *State of the world's children*

Valley, S. (1999) Teachers in South Africa: Between fiscal austerity and getting learning right *Quarterly Review of Education and Training in South Africa,* 6, 10-23

Valley, S. and Dalamba, Y. (1999) *Racism, Racial Integration and Deracialiasation in South African Public Secondary Schools.* Pretoria, South African Human Rights Commission

Wainaina, B. (2005) How to write about Africa *Granta,* 92, 91- 95

Williams, P. (2004) Britain and Africa after the cold war: beyond damage limitation? in I. Taylor and P. Williams (eds) *Africa in international politics: external involvement on the continent.* London: Routledge

Wilson, D. Greenspan, R. and Wilson, C. (1989) Knowledge about AIDS and self-reported behaviour among Zimbabwean secondary school pupils *Social Science and Medicine,* 28, 957-961

World Bank (2000) *Federal Republic of Nigeria: water supply and sanitation interim strategy note* November 2000

Index